Robert Kite's

SUCCESSFUL

CANADIAN
RETIREMENT PLAN

It worked for him

It can work for you!

RETIRE RICH!

A LuLu.com published Book

Cover design by specialist...
www.4npc.com

2

ISBN: 978-1-4357-0569-2

Publisher: Lulu.com

Acknowledgements

I would like to thank the following for their generous help with this book.

Val Gee, writer and editor for explaining the issues and showing me how the writing industry works; my darling wife, for the lonely life she endured while I shut myself away for months-on-end; Neil Prime-Coote, R. G. D. of www.4npc.comWeb Design and Photos, for his invaluable help in the preparation and execution of the outside cover.

And to the late Robert Kite Senior (1874 - 1961), a gentleman and a grandfather whose compassion and kindness formed fond childhood memories that motivated me into doing this for *him* and Canadians everywhere.

Robert Kite's Successful **CANADIAN RETIREMENT PLAN**

by Robert Kite

ABOUT THE BOOK

To everybody's great horror average people around the world are learning that they can no longer rely on a company or government pension to give them a secure and comfortable retirement - even if they've paid into it for years.

Will you be a *poor* senior?

At last, here is an easy-to-read book that addresses that problem. It is written for everyone from 25-50 who wants to learn how to quickly plan for a rich and happy retirement. By following the easy steps, readers will experience a real buzz as the years roll by and their nest egg grows.

This book arose uniquely out of personal experience.

Twenty or so years ago the writer was an ordinary guy enjoying his work in hotel and institutional management. At that time during his forties, he was shocked to become aware that like many of his friends, he too had a large mortgage, big credit card and car payments but with just a small handful of RRSPs for his future pension.

As he writes, "Unless we took drastic measures immediately, my wife Polly and I would outlive our money, and experience our "golden years" in poverty."

Robert successfully adapted a plan that he used in his business career and now he and Polly are debt free and have more than enough money to live their retirement dream in comfort.

He now shares that successful plan with his readers.

Yes, in a unique way, *Robert Kite's* book addresses the looming problem of the pension shortfall and provides practical solutions.

Employers struggle to maintain their financial bottom line in the face of an advancing group of baby boomers and are making drastic cuts to staff pension plans.

The Canadian pension fund is in danger from the same problem and with an aging population it too may be unable to provide adequate pensions to make up the difference.

Is it too late for the average Canadian to achieve a secure retirement? Is it too late to start a retirement fund? The many thousands of people who presently face a retirement with disappointment and frustration can find hope from this book.

Like Robert and Polly, they too will have a chance to enjoy a retirement that they deserve and so avoid the dread of outliving their money.

Women's issues in particular are explored in a full chapter with the help of real research sources. They range from discussions with women of different ages and financial circumstances to current news reports and the updated and expanded Statistics Canada report, *Women in Canada: A Gender-based Statistical Report*, released March 13, 2006.

Featured are other actions that women can take to *secure* their finances, and single women in particular are shown that they too can look forward to a happy retirement on a single income.

DISCLAIMER
While every effort has been made to ensure true and faithful content, the author is not responsible for the outcome of any discussed retirement or savings plan and success is not guaranteed. Further, the author has no financial qualifications and his retirement planning experiences are only suggestions. Consult a qualified financial adviser.

Robert Kite's

Successful
Canadian Retirement Plan

by
Robert Kite

CONTENTS

Page

Robert Kite's
SUCCESSFUL
CANADIAN
RETIREMENT PLAN

by
Robert Kite

ABOUT THE AUTHOR

Robert Kite acts under the name of David Coote. He has verses published under the name Jack Churchill.

Robert Kite went to drama school in London, England as a boy and was immediately signed to star in five feature movies. Additional film work amounted to around thirty movies. Robert has appeared in over 300 TV productions for BBC and others and his theatre experience includes the West End stage, Shakespeare and repertory theatre. Work colleagues include Cary Grant, Ingrid Bergman, and Peter Ustinov.

www.imdb.com search david coote.

His acting career took him throughout Europe until he was drafted for National Service in 1958. His 2-years in the Royal Air Force saw him fly jet fighters and he was posted to Cyprus for a brief combat mission.

At about that time Robert bred Chow Chow dogs and took three second place awards at the world famous Cruft's Dog Show in London.

Robert entered the hotel business in 1964 with Grand Metropolitan hotels in London and the Channel Islands. His training continued with Cornell University, New York and Four Seasons Hotels.

His General Manager appointments include the Grand Hotel, Jersey and the Eaton Hall Hotel & Conference Centre in Ontario, Canada, which he founded in 1978 for Seneca College.

His many personal house guests include, The late Princess Margaret, Johnny Mathis, The Carpenters, Michael Jackson, Juliet Prowse, James Stewart, Milton Berle, Ronald Reagan, Lester Pearson, Pierre Trudeau, Andre Kostelanetz, Mama Cass Elliott, Jack Lemmon, Dr Charles Best, Helen Hayes, Chief Dan George, Alexei Kosygin, Rudolf Byng and Sergei Ozawa.

As President of the Canadian Hospitality Institute, in 1985 he and his wife dined with the Queen of England and Prince Philip. During that period he gave many public speeches across Canada.

In 1986 Robert was honored by the Spanish School of Hotel Management with a professorship and was invited to design and present a series of lectures at their college in Barcelona, Spain.

His institutional experience includes senior administrative appointments with the Guy's & St Thomas' Hospitals, London and King's College London.

In 1991 he was appointed visiting professor for the Hotel, Business and Personnel Management program at St Margaret University, Edinburgh.

During his current retirement years he is performing an administrative function with a Private Investigators' office in Toronto. He also acts in TV Commercials; conducts hotel and retail store audits; markets himself worldwide as a relief hotel manager and writes novels. He is a 30-year member of ACTRA, (Alliance of Canadian Television and Radio Artists).

Robert enjoys cooking, playing golf, fishing, shopping, traveling and taking his wife for drives in his classic Jaguar.

His credentials to write this book with some authority come from his financial planning experience used in his professional work as well as his own personal *Retirement Plan* that proved successful after a trial of over twenty years.

His previous publications include many professional papers and reports for Guys and St Thomas' Hospitals and the Association of University Teachers in his honorary post as Recruitment Secretary. His financial reports were published by King's College London.

His verses titled *East Lothian Has it All* were accepted for publication in Scottish Poets edited by Suzy Goodall (Arrival Press 1995). Other publications include verses for Carlton greetings cards.

Charts & Spreadsheets

This section contains twelve spreadsheets that I personally devised to help me set up and maintain control of our retirement plan.

They all are under the heading *"Plan your Retirement – Don't Outlive Your Money!"* This was intended to regularly remind me to do just that – to plan my retirement and stick to it so as not to outlive our money!

I needed to be able to estimate approximately how much I would need to have in a savings or pension account when I was at retirement age. Enough so that Polly and I could live the sort of life that we wanted.

To do this we needed to estimate what our monthly spend would be. Once we knew this then the yearly figure would be easy to calculate. Next, we would need to compute the savings necessary (which would be our nest egg or money tree) that would generate the yearly amount we needed to live on.

We would need to add in the pensions that we hoped that we would receive from government plans. I say, *"hoped"* because even all those years ago, a family relative was predicting that when I would be old enough to retire it would be doubtful if governments would have enough money left in the pension pot for everybody.

I then had the idea that if we were debt free at retirement age then we would need considerably less to live on. So I needed to draw a graph or a chart that would show me what our mortgage (and other debts) was and then develop a long-term workable plan that would take care of the collapse of the debt within a period of twenty or so years.

So you see, rather than just guess these numbers, it was necessary to do some time-consuming work using honest numbers that would materialise if my plan were to succeed. To put them on paper in an organised fashion gave me a picture to look at – the complete picture if you like.

I am not suggesting that you use all of the charts but you may find some of them useful in preparing your own personal retirement plan.

Charts & Spreadsheets

Chart # 1

Chart # 1 is called the Personal Net Worth Assessment Register and you will find that this chart is referred to in the book.

As the book is about retirement you may think that it would be useful to know how much pension you will need to live on when you get there. I will show you how to assess this.

I urge you to consider the entire project as a journey – a journey to your dream. So, as with any journey, to plot the course with any degree of accuracy, you need to establish the point from where you are starting.

You need to have a general idea as to how much money you have now and that will help you estimate how much more you need to save, but more of that later.

On the opposite page there is an example of a spreadsheet style that you could use to assess your own personal NET worth, which is a fancy way of saying that you can estimate with a fair degree of accuracy the value of everything that you own. I used a chart like this and in fact I still do. Simply put, what you are doing here is taking something that you own such as a car - and writing down how much you think the present day value is. Let's say $5,000. That will tell you the GROSS value.

If you owe any money on the car, that would be referred to as a debt. To find the NET value, you need to deduct the amount of the debt from the gross value. Let's suppose that you owe $2,000. You deduct the debt of $2,000 from the $5,000. That leaves $3,000.

Thus, the NET value of your car to you is $3,000.

To establish your TOTAL NET WORTH, you will need to do this with everything that you own. A grid such as the one depicted on the opposite page is a simple way of organising the items as you go through the process. If you have never done this exercise before, you may be surprised as to how much money you are really worth.

PLAN YOUR RETIREMENT - DON'T OUTLIVE YOUR MONEY! / KITE
CHART # 1
PERSONAL NET WORTH ASSESSMENT REGISTER
NAME: _____
PERSONAL ASSETS & LIABILITIES - EXAMPLE ONLY
DATE: December 31, xxxx: YEAR 1 of my Retirement Plan
ESTIMATED PERSONAL NET WORTH: $664,225

		CURRENT ESTIMATED VALUE	CURRENT DEBT OWING	NET WORTH
REAL ESTATE	Real Estate # 1	450,000	200,000	250,000
	Real Estate # 2	300,000	200,000	100,000
MAJOR ITEMS	Car # 1	30,000	20,000	10,000
	Car # 2	12,000		12,000
	Boat # 1	40,000	25,000	15,000
STOCKS & SHARES	Blue chip # 1	5,000		5,000
	Blue chip # 2	8,000		8,000
	Energy shares	10,000		10,000
	Gold Shares	10,000		10,000
PENSION INVESTMENTS	RRSP'S # 1	85,000		85,000
	RRSP'S # 2	45,000		45,000
	INVESTMENTS	10,000		10,000
	INVESTMENTS	5,000		5,000
BANK SAVINGS	ACCOUNT # 1	5,000		5,000
	ACOUNT # 2	3,000		3,000
OTHER ACCOUNTS	CHEQUING	500		500
	CREDIT CARD # 1		4,500	(4,500)
	CREDIT CARD # 2		3,000	(3,000)
	LINE OF CREDIT		8,000	(8,000)
OTHER DEBTS				
CASH ON HAND	PERSON # 1	150		150
	PERSON # 2	75		75
ANTIQUES & PAINTINGS	PAINTING # 1	3,000		3,000
	CLOCK	15,000		15,000
				0
FURNITURE	HOME	50,000		50,000
	2nd Property	25,000		25,000
JEWELRY	PERSONAL	8,000		8,000
				0
FURS	PERSONAL	5,000		5,000
TOTAL		1,124,725	460,500	664,225

Notes: i. This chart shows a list of all personal assets and liabilities as an example.
ii. The Current Estimated Value or *gross* worth is approximate and amounts to $1,124,725.
iii. The Current Debt Owing is estimated to be in the amount of $460,500.
iv. The Net Worth (NW) is the Current Value less any Debt Owing. The total NW is $664,225.
v. Re-calculate the asset values annually to assess your total worth.

Charts & Spreadsheets

Chart # 2

Chart # 2 demonstrates the power of compounding, which is a fancy way of describing the rapidity of growth when referring to money. The other side of the coin is that when you *owe* money that power of compounding works *against* you. It is important that you know this even if you do not clearly understand it.

The knowledge that something is working against you may just be the catalyst that motivates you to reduce your borrowing and to consider seriously about paying off your debt more quickly than you otherwise might have done.

You can see by the chart that the sum of $3,500 grows more rapidly towards the end of the life of the investment. Similarly, when you owe money, the impact of your monthly payments is not felt very much until the end of the life of the mortgage is near. Then the monthly payments really take effect – big time.

But let's get back to the investment. The interest rate here is very important and the figure of 9½ % is academic really, but it is not an impossible figure to attain, especially when investing your savings over such a long period as thirty-five years.

Perhaps when you study this chart at length you realise the great benefit of starting on your retirement plan as early in life as possible.

It is also vital that you leave the investment to mature *undisturbed*. If you were to break the term of the investment and take out the cash, even if only for a year or so, and were to re-invest it, the end result would be entirely different. The overall loss to the ultimate value of your fund could be considerable.

PLAN YOUR RETIREMENT-DON'T OUTLIVE YOUR MONEY! / KITE

CHART # 2

INVESTMENT WITH A FUND MANAGER - EXAMPLE
SAVE $3,500 JUST ONCE - AND INVEST IT FOR 35 YEARS

Average annual interest:		9.5%

YEAR	ORIGINAL INVESTMENT	ANNUAL INTEREST EARNED	YEAR END BALANCE
1	**3,500**	333	3,833
2		364	4,197
3		399	4,595
4		437	5,032
5		478	5,510
6		523	6,033
7		573	6,606
8		628	7,234
9		687	7,921
10		753	8,674
11		824	9,498
12		902	10,400
13		988	11,388
14		1,082	12,470
15		1,185	13,655
16		1,297	14,952
17		1,420	16,372
18		1,555	17,928
19		1,703	19,631
20		1,865	21,496
21		2,042	23,538
22		2,236	25,774
23		2,449	28,222
24		2,681	30,903
25		2,936	33,839
26		3,215	37,054
27		3,520	40,574
28		3,855	44,429
29		4,221	48,649
30		4,622	53,271
31		5,061	58,332
32		5,542	63,873
33		6,068	69,941
34		6,644	76,586
35		7,276	**83,861**

NOTES:

i. This example demonstrates how a one-time investment of $3,500 saved with a fund manager within a GSTSF, could grow to $83.8k in a period of 35-years.

ii. Remember, there are many older women living in poverty. If you do this at aged 35, the reward could be a happy 70th birthday!

iii. Notice how the Annual Interest Earned balloons from just $478 in Year-5 to $4.6k in Year-30 and to a huge $7.2k in Year-35.

iv. The immense power of compounding is clearly demonstrated, which is why it is so important to start your Retirement Plan without delay.

v. The great value of *leaving your savings untouched* for as long as possible is also clearly seen. Perodic withdrawing and re-investing would not produce the same results.

vi. $10k invested once with the same conditions could earn $240k in 35-years.

GSTSF = Government Sponsored Tax Sheltered Fund

Charts & Spreadsheets

Chart # 3

This chart adds an interesting dimension to Chart # 2 in that it assumes that you were so impressed with what a mere $3,500 could grow to you would wish to do more.

This chart provides you with that opportunity and amply rewards you for making a yearly sacrifice of $3,500 over a period of 35-years. The end result could be a tantalising nine hundred thousand dollars!

Again, the immense power of compounding does the work for you but the investments must not be disturbed over the entire term if you are to enjoy the optimum reward.

PLAN YOUR RETIREMENT - DON'T OUTLIVE YOUR MONEY / KITE
CHART # 3
INVESTMENT WITH A FUND MANAGER - EXAMPLE
SAVE $3,500 - EVERY YEAR THROUGH 35-YEARS
CHART # 3

Average yearly interest:			9.5%

YEAR	YEARLY INVESTMENT	BALANCE	ANNUAL INTEREST EARNED	YEAR-END BALANCE
1	**3,500**	3,500	333	3,833
2	3,500	7,333	697	8,029
3	3,500	11,529	1,095	12,624
4	3,500	16,124	1,532	17,656
5	3,500	21,156	2,010	23,166
6	3,500	26,666	2,533	29,199
7	3,500	32,699	3,106	35,806
8	3,500	39,306	3,734	43,040
9	3,500	46,540	4,421	50,961
10	3,500	54,461	5,174	59,635
11	3,500	63,135	5,998	69,133
12	3,500	72,633	6,900	79,533
13	3,500	83,033	7,888	90,921
14	3,500	94,421	8,970	103,391
15	3,500	106,891	10,155	117,045
16	3,500	120,545	11,452	131,997
17	3,500	135,497	12,872	148,369
18	3,500	151,869	14,428	166,297
19	3,500	169,797	16,131	185,928
20	3,500	189,428	17,996	207,423
21	3,500	210,923	20,038	230,961
22	3,500	234,461	22,274	256,735
23	3,500	260,235	24,722	284,957
24	3,500	288,457	27,403	315,861
25	3,500	319,361	30,339	349,700
26	3,500	353,200	33,554	386,754
27	3,500	390,254	37,074	427,328
28	3,500	430,828	40,929	471,757
29	3,500	475,257	45,149	520,406
30	3,500	523,906	49,771	573,677
31	3,500	577,177	54,832	632,009
32	3,500	635,509	60,373	695,883
33	3,500	699,383	66,441	765,824
34	3,500	769,324	73,086	842,410
35	3,500	845,910	80,361	**926,271**

Notes:

i. This example demonstrates how saving $3,500 each year for 35 years and investing it within an GSTSF with a fund manager with certain conditions could grow to nearly $1m.

ii. If you start doing this at age 35, your retirement might be the envy of many people.

iii. If you save just $2k each year, a 9.5% yield could provide you with $562k in 35 years

iv. Notice how the *Annual Interest Earned* balloons from about $2k in Year 5 to about $50k in Year 30 and a huge $80k in Year 35.

v. The immense power of compounding interest is clearly demonstrated which is why it is important to start your Retirement Plan without delay.

vi. The importance of *leaving your savings untouched* for as long as possible is also clearly seen. Periodic withdrawing and reinvesting could not produce the same results.

GSTSF = Government Sponsored Tax Sheltered Fund

Charts & Spreadsheets

Chart # 4

This is a fun chart really and I think that my tongue was firmly in my cheek when I prepared this one.

We are all guilty of impulsive buying and why not? So long as we are not spending our retirement pension money!

The fascinating subject of impulsive buying is explored at length in Chapter 3 - *A woman's Perspective.*

It might appear that in my opinion, only women are guilty of this enjoyable past time. That was certainly not my intention as of course nearly everyone practices this habit. I see this happening every time I visit a shopping mall or an airport and really, I find it quite worrying.

The important point here is to know what you can afford to spend impulsively without denying yourself the happy retirement that you dream of.

The chart assumes that you spend $100.00 every month unnecessarily and illustrates what the result might be if the money was redirected into a retirement pension fund.

With a bit of good luck and determination a twenty-year habit could grow to nearly $100,000.00!

PLAN YOUR RETIREMENT-DON'T OUTLIVE YOUR MONEY / KITE
CHART # 4
IMPULSIVE BUYING SUBSTITUTE - over $240,000 in 30-years!
MONTHLY SPEND OF $100 FOR 20 -YEARS
Average Interest Rate: 10%

	Monthly Savings	Prev Yr Totals	Add Interest	Yr End Totals
Year - 1	1,200		120	1,320
2	1,200	2,520	252	2,772
3	1,200	3,972	397	4,369
4	1,200	5,569	557	7,326
5	1,200	8,526	853	9,379
6	1,200	10,579	1,058	11,637
7	1,200	12,837	1,284	15,320
8	1,200	16,520	1,652	18,172
9	1,200	19,372	1,937	21,310
10	1,200	22,510	2,251	25,960
11	1,200	27,160	2,716	29,877
12	1,200	31,077	3,108	34,184
13	1,200	35,384	3,538	40,123
14	1,200	41,323	4,132	45,455
15	1,200	46,655	4,665	51,320
16	1,200	52,520	5,252	58,972
17	1,200	60,172	6,017	66,190
18	1,200	67,390	6,739	74,129
19	1,200	75,329	7,533	84,061
20	1,200	85,261	8,526	**93,788**

This is an example of how you can use your impulsive monthly buying spend of $100 and give it to your fund manager.

Notes:

i.   The actual amount spent with your fund manager every month is $100.
ii. The actual amount put aside over 20-years will amount to $24,000.
iii. At the end of 20-years, under certain conditions the interest earned at 10% could be nearly $70,000.
iv. The total amount in your account could be over $93,000.
v.   If you choose to leave the $93k untouched for a further ten years and add nothing more to it. at 10% per annum it could grow to $243,000.

Charts & Spreadsheets

Chart # 5

I call Chart # 5 *"Monthly Budget – Living Costs during Working Years."*

When I first started to think about preparing a retirement plan I felt the need to know more about our spending habits. I think most people have very little idea as to how much they spend each month and we were no different.

In truth, it really doesn't matter what you spend each week or month providing that it is less than you earn!

But more than that - I wanted to see if we could possibly cut down our monthly spend and so have a little extra left over. It we could do that then at the end of each year we could afford to make an extra mortgage payment. The bank told us that if we did that, over a period of several years we would save ourselves many thousands of dollars. That was the incentive we were looking for.

And so the monthly budget sheet was born. I still use it today although for a different reason. After a career managing properties of one sort or another, I am in the habit of monitoring income and expenditures and so I continue to enjoy this happy pastime. It takes just a few minutes each week and provides me with a complete picture as to where our money comes from and where it goes.

PLAN YOUR RETIREMENT-DON'T OUTLIVE YOUR MONEY! / KITE

CHART # 5

MONTHLY BUDGET - LIVING COSTS DURING WORKING YEARS

MONTH: April (Month #4)

EXAMPLE ONLY

| TOTAL MONTHLY BUDGET: 3,425 | | | Total budget for the year brought forward: 10,275 | | | | | Total Budget for the year to date carried forward: 13,700 | | | | | |

MONTHLY BUDGET:	1200	500	400	425	150	100	50	50	200	50	50	50	200	Misc.
DETAILS OF ITEM PURCHASED	Home mortgage payment or rent	Home taxes water/heat light telephones	Food including soft drinks cleaners & soaps	Auto payments & insurance	Auto Gas/Wash plates road toll auto service	Restaurant & Coffee Shops	Medical Prescripts	Home Items New items light bulbs, plants, etc.	Personal Bus/train clothes shoes hair, etc.	Wine Liquor & Beer	Dental	Hobbies	Vacations & Trips	Capital items & one-time purchases
Day of Month														
1 — Mortgage Payment, including Taxes	970													
1 — Electricity Bill		70												
1 — Heating Bill		300												
1 — Water Bill		45												
1 — House/Property Taxes		230												
3 — Groceries			77											
5 — Telephone Company		62												
6 — Bus / train fares									25					
6 — The Beer Store										22				
6 — Liquor Store										17				
10 — Car Payment				310										
10 — Gasoline & Car Wash					34									
10 — Bus/train fares									25					
12 — Sweater & Jeans									38					
12 — Cash & Carry - Food			57											
14 — Paint and brushes								27						
14 — Light Bulbs								16						
25 — Groceries			48						25					
26 — Bus/train fares									25					
27 — Car Insurance				110										
28 — Auto Service, Gasoline & Car Wash					236									
29 — Restaurant						45								
29 — Wine Store										9				
30 — Groceries			85							48				
ITEM COST TOTALS:	970	707	267	420	270	45	0	43	138	48				

| **TOTAL MONTHLY SPEND: 2,908** | | | Total spend year to date b/f from last month: 8,124 | | | | | Total spend year to date carried forward: 11,032 | | | | | |

	1200	500	400	425	150	100	50	50	200	50	50	50	200	Misc.
Brought forward from last month:	3,600	1,475	535	1,275	230	115	26	150	120	144	125	200	0	400
New balance year to date to carry forward:	4,570	2,182	802	1,695	500	160	26	193	258	192	125	200	0	400

NOTES: i. The numbers used are examples only.

ii. Use column headings that suit your own circumstances.

iii. Carrying the amounts forward each month provides you with an instant Year-End total in December.

iv. The monthly budget is $3,425. The spend this month was $2,908 leaving a surplus of $517.

v. This month's surplus of $517 should be used as an extra payment against the mortgage.

Charts & Spreadsheets

Chart # 6

This chart came out a plan I developed to ensure that our mortgage was paid off in full by a certain date – in my case, when I was 65. In fact, due to unexpected circumstances, it was paid off when I was 63.

But the point here is that to achieve your goal of a happy, debt-free retirement you might think it sensible to measure how many years you have left in which to pay down your mortgage, and really, when you break it down into years, somehow the goal appears to be more achievable.

I compiled the years into 5-year blocks. That way, every five years I was able to assess our performance and make any adjustment necessary so as to accomplish the objective.

Of course, you can easily compile your own chart, but I thought that to include this one here might be a helpful tool to get you started.

PLAN YOUR RETIREMENT-DON'T OUTLIVE YOUR MONEY! / KITE
CHART # 6
20-YEAR MORTGAGE PLAN (Example)
Mortgage value: $130,000
Interest Rate: 6 %
Payment Years Remaining: 20
Current age of Mortgagor: 45

Age of Mortgagor	45	46	47	48	49	50
	Year	Year	Year	Year	Year	Year
1st 5-Year Block	0	1	2	3	4	5
	130,000	126,529	122,844	118,932	114,779	110,370

Age of Mortgagor	51	52	53	54	55
	Year	Year	Year	Year	Year
2nd 5-Year Block	6	7	8	9	10
	105,688	100,718	95,441	89,839	83,891

Age of Mortgagor	56	57	58	59	60
	Year	Year	Year	Year	Year
3rd 5-Year Block	11	12	13	14	15
	77,576	70,872	63,755	56,198	48,175

Age of Mortgagor	61	62	63	64	65
	Year	Year	Year	Year	Year
4th 5-Year Block	16	17	18	19	20
	39,658	30,615	21,014	10,822	0

Notes:

i.   The mortgage plan as shown here is an example only.

ii. The year "0" represents the year in which the mortgage is arranged.

iii. The objective is to have the mortgage paid off by year 20.

iv. The interest or cost to borrow $130,000 over a 20 year period will amount to $93,527.

v.   The combined principal & interest payments to borrow $130,000 will be $223,527.

vi. Under certain conditions, if *extra payments* can be made during each of the twenty years, huge savings can be made and the mortgage can be paid off much sooner than the due date.

vii. Under certain conditions, *weekly* payments can benefit you more than monthly payments with the result that your mortgage will be paid off years earlier and you can make huge savings.

viii. Be sure to shop around for the best mortgage that suits your particular need. Ask questions.

Charts & Spreadsheets

Chart # 7

The earlier Chart #5 provided a basic grid for using as a guide to monitor your spending during your working years.

Here, Chart # 7 is the same idea but is intended for you to use during your retirement years.

The reason that I include it is that as I am in my retirement years I have a pretty good idea as to what we spend our money on. I presume that you may still be working and therefore will only be able to guess much of this information.

Of course, as with all of the charts the numbers are fictitious and are offered for guidance only.

You will notice several differences. Some of these could be caused due to our being empty nesters. Also, as you no doubt will have heard from parents or grandparents, as we are older, Polly and I tend to eat less. We also spend less on daily travel, clothes and jewellery. That leaves more for international travel, which is really our main pleasure throughout the year.

PLAN YOUR RETIREMENT-DON'T OUTLIVE YOUR MONEY!/ KITE
CHART # 7
RETIREMENT BUDGET - MONTHLY LIVING COSTS
MONTH: June (Month # 6)
EXAMPLE ONLY

TOTAL MONTHLY BUDGET: 2,480   Total budget for the year brought forward: 12,400   Total Budget for the year to date carried forward: 14,880

Day of Month	MONTHLY BUDGET / DETAILS OF ITEM PURCHASED	Home mortgage payment or rent	Home taxes water/heat light telephones	Food including soft drinks cleaners & soaps	Auto payments & insurance	Auto Gas/Wash plates road toll auto service	Restaurant & Coffee Shops	Medical Prescripts	Home Items New items light bulbs, plants, etc.	Personal clothes shoes cleaning hair, etc.	Wine Liquor & Beer	Dental	Hobbies	Vacations & Trips	Misc. Capital items & one-time purchases
		0	700	500	100	130	250	30	50	300	120	50	50	200	
1	Condominium Maintenance inc. Water Heat Hydro		450												
1	Condominium Taxes		175												
3	Groceries			140											
5	Telephone Company		62												
6	The Beer Store										24				
6	Liquor Store										34				
10	Gasoline & Car Wash					47									
12	Pants & shirt									55					
12	Cash & Carry - Food			90											
14	Batteries								12						
14	Light Bulbs								16						
25	Groceries			88											
27	Car Insurance				96										
28	Auto Service, Gasoline & Car Wash					52									
29	Restaurant						120								
30	Wine Store										24				
30	Groceries			105											
	ITEM COST TOTALS:	0	687	423	96	99	120	0	28	55	82				

TOTAL MONTHLY SPEND: 1,590   Total spend brought forward from last month: 11,877   Total spend year to date carried forward: 13,467

	Home mortgage payment or rent	Home taxes	Food	Auto payments	Auto Gas/Wash	Restaurant	Medical Prescripts	Home Items	Personal	Wine	Dental	Hobbies	Vacations	Misc.
Brought forward from last month:	0	3,450	2,400	480	510	980	48	235	1,265	525	654	542	0	788
New balance year to date to carry forward:	0	4,137	2,823	576	609	1,100	48	263	1,320	607	654	542	0	788

NOTES: i. This monthly budget is for use in your retirement years and demonstrates the changes in your lifestyle. The numbers used are examples only.
ii. Notice the lack of any mortage or rent payments. Also the lack of any car payment or regular travel costs to get to work.
iii. In line with the Retirement Plan, at this stage in your life your monthly living costs should be minimal.
iv. Use column headings that suit your own circumstances.
v. Carrying the amounts forward each month provides you with an instant Year-End total in December.

Charts & Spreadsheets

Chart # 8

This financial chart was designed to tell me how our savings were doing in terms of growth.

I knew that some years would be better than others and by assembling them together in a grid it would be easy for me to compare year on year performances.

The numbers are entirely fictitious and are provided for demonstration purposes only. However, hopefully by reviewing the format you will be able to readily prepare your own chart to suit your particular needs.

PLAN YOUR RETIREMENT-DON'T OUTLIVE YOUR MONEY!/KITE

CHART # 8

PERSONAL INVESTMENTS & SAVINGS RECORD - YR ON YR VARIANCES

NAME: Jane & John Doe

REGISTERED RETIREMENT SAVINGS PLAN (RRSP) FUNDS

GUARANTEED INCOME CERTIFICATES

STOCKS AND SHARES / MUTUAL FUNDS

YEAR ON YEAR VARIANCES

	Year 1	Year 2	Year 3	Year 4	Year 5
EXAMPLE ONLY					
RRSP FUND # 1: $5,000. Fixed interest rate of 2% per year.	5,000	5,100	5,202	5,306	5,412
RRSP FUND # 2: A fund (mainly bonds) considered fairly low risk.	1,000	1,050	1,082	1,092	1,169
RRSP FUND # 3: A fund with a slightly higher risk level.	3,000	3,120	3,276	3,374	3,576
RRSP FUND # 4: A high risk fund.	4,000	5,040	6,250	4,555	5,599
RRSP FUND # 5: A mutual fund with medium risk.	3,000	3,090	3,245	3,358	3,509
GIC # 1: Accelerated Rate type of Guaranteed Income Certificate.	2,000	2,050	2,103	2,164	2,250
GIC # 2: A 5-year GIC paying 3.85 % interest each year.	5,000	5,193	5,392	5,600	5,816
SHARES # 1: Energy sector stocks.	3,000	3,360	3,931	3,655	4,167
SHARES # 2: Precious Metals sector stocks.	2,000	2,060	2,101	2,143	2,228
SHARES # 3: Real Estate sector stocks.	2,000	2,360	2,643	2,775	3,219
SHARES # 4: Financial sector stocks	2,000	2,120	2,290	2,358	2,500
SHARES # 5: Pharmaceutical sector stocks	2,000	2,280	2,554	2,783	3228
TOTAL	**34,000**	**36,823**	**40,069**	**39,163**	**42,673**
Year on year variance in dollar amounts		2,823	3,246	-906	3,510
Variance percentage		8.3%	8.8%	-2.3%	9.0%
Total growth for the 5-year period expressed in dollars					8,673
Total growth for the 5-year period expressed as a percentage					25.5%

Notes:
  i. This chart shows a five-year block as an example only.
  ii. The yearly columns contain the annual values.
  iii. Year #4 was not a good year for growth. Some sectors actually experienced negative growth.
  v. The year-on-year percentage variances reflect the increase or decrease in the annual amounts.
  vi. It is important to remain diversified. Your portfolio should contain a varied mix of investments with varied risk levels.

Charts & Spreadsheets

Chart # 9

Did you ever stop to think how much you are worth? In terms of money I mean. You may be pleasantly surprised.

Personally, I don't think it really matters how much you are worth, the important thing is to have enough money so that you can afford to do the things that you want to without worrying.

But if you are in mid life and saving for your retirement you may want to monitor your savings and each month estimate the values as part of your plan – to see that you are on track. To obtain the full picture however, you will need to know the value of all of your assets, as this detail will be vital when you come to retire.

The value of any real estate you own, particularly your home or primary residence will usually vary from year to year, sometimes very considerably. A major increase in it's value due to market forces may provide you with such a large (tax free) capital gain that retirement may come to you earlier that you had expected.

Chart # 9 is meant to help you track your personal total wealth while prompting you to review the current values of all of the items.

PLAN YOUR RETIREMENT-DON'T OUTLIVE YOUR MONEY!/ KITE
CHART # 9
NET WORTH - YEAR ON YEAR VARIANCES
NAME: Jane & John Doe

EXAMPLE ONLY	Year 1	Year 2	Year 3	Year 4	Year 5
REAL ESTATE	350,000	355,000	385,000	385,000	420,000
MAJOR ITEMS	37,000	35,000	30,000	25,000	30,000
STOCKS & SHARES	33,000	36,000	40,000	38,000	41,000
PENSION INVESTMENTS	145,000	147,000	153,000	154,000	160,000
BANK SAVINGS	8,000	5,000	5,000	7,000	5,000
OTHER ACCOUNTS - Line of credit: amount of debt	(15,000)	(12,000)	(9,000)	(7,000)	(5,000)
OTHER DEBTS	0	(700)	(500)	(300)	(1,000)
CASH ON HAND	225	150	200	150	300
ANTIQUES & PAINTINGS - Replacement Value	18,000	20,000	21,000	21,000	25,000
FURNITURE - Replacement value	75,000	75,000	60,000	50,000	45,000
JEWELRY - Replacement value	8,000	8,000	9,000	9,000	10,000
FURS - Replacement value	5,000	4,000	4,000	4,000	5000
TOTAL	664,225	672,450	697,700	685,850	735,300
Year-on-year variance in dollar amounts		8,225	25,250	-11,850	49,450
Variance percentage		1.2%	3.8%	-1.7%	7.2%

Notes: i. This chart shows a five-year block as an example only.
ii. The values in each of the yearly columns are net worth amounts.
iii. Year #4 saw negative growth. This was due to a major correction that occurred in many of the investment sectors.
iv. The year-on-year variance is expressed in dollar amounts.
v. The year-on-year *percentage* variance reflects the increase or decrease in the net worth as a percentage.
vi. To remain consistent, it is suggested that the values be determined at the same time each year - i.e., December 31.

Charts & Spreadsheets

Chart # 10

If you are currently in your forties or fifties and have done very little about saving for your retirement you may feel there is little hope that you can retire early, or indeed if you will be able to retire at all.

Do not despair. It will not be easy, but take a look at Chart # 10.

Depending on your specific circumstances, you may feel that $250 is an amount of money that you could afford to put away every month. If so, with patience, a good fund manager and a bit of good luck, after about 20-years you could have a nest egg of over $160,000.

That sort of money would give your retirement years an extra $1,000 each month for a period of over 13-years. That could make the difference between living in poverty or comfort.

The object here is not to provide false hope to those in need of genuine help but to show that where there's a will there's a way. If you like, it merely provides another option to consider if you have a real desire to possess a decent pension plan in your older years.

...AN YOUR RETIREMENT-DON'T OUTLIVE YOUR MONEY!/ KITE

...HART # 10

...TE STARTERS' INVESTMENT GROWTH CHART

...nnual Contribution Amount: $3,000
...erage Annual Yield: 8%
...ntribution period: 21 years

EXAMPLE ONLY

age	annual amount invested	amount saved including interest	interest earned in year 1
50	3000	3240	240
51	3000	6739	499
52	3000	10518	779
53	3000	14600	1081
54	3000	19008	1408
55	3000	23768	1761
56	3000	28910	2141
57	3000	34463	2553
58	3000	40460	2997
59	3000	46936	3477
60	3000	53931	3995
61	3000	61486	4555
62	3000	69645	5159
63	3000	78456	5812
64	3000	87973	6516
65	3000	98251	7278
66	3000	109350	8100
67	3000	121339	8988
68	3000	134286	9947
69	3000	148269	10983
70	3000	163370	12102

$63,000

NOTES:

i.   In this example the investor starts saving at age 50. By their early 70s, they can have over $163k in their fund.

ii. The investor will actually save only $63k of their own money but will earn $100,370 in interest.

iii. The upper number in each group represents the total amount saved in that year.

iv. The lower number in each group represents the total interest earned in that year.

v.   Note that in Year 1 only $240 interest is earned while in Year 21, $12,102 interest is earned.

vi. The immense power of compounding is demonstrated in the chart.

vii. The average interest rate of 8% is achieved by the fund manager investing at higher risk v

viii.The late starter will likely need to continue working until tl

ix. The chart demonstrates to the late starter that with self-constraint and regular contributions, a retirement nest egg can still be possible.

x.   The chart is an example only and investment yields may be higher or lower depending on varying conditions.

Charts & Spreadsheets

Chart # 11

Chart # 11 is not so much as a working tool to use but rather an informative instrument plucked from the Statistics Canada files published by them in 2006.

The chart is about the average retirement savings in dollars and illustrates that in 2004, within the group earning between $40,000-$60,000, women were found to have been putting away in RRSP's more money for their retirement than men.

I'm not sure what else to say other than to raise the issue so that we can be aware of the sorts of things that we all should be doing.

PLAN YOUR RETIREMENT-DON'T OUTLIVE YOUR MONEY!/ KITE
CHART # 11
2004 STATISTICS BLOCK CHART

Retirement Savings through RRSPs and RPPs

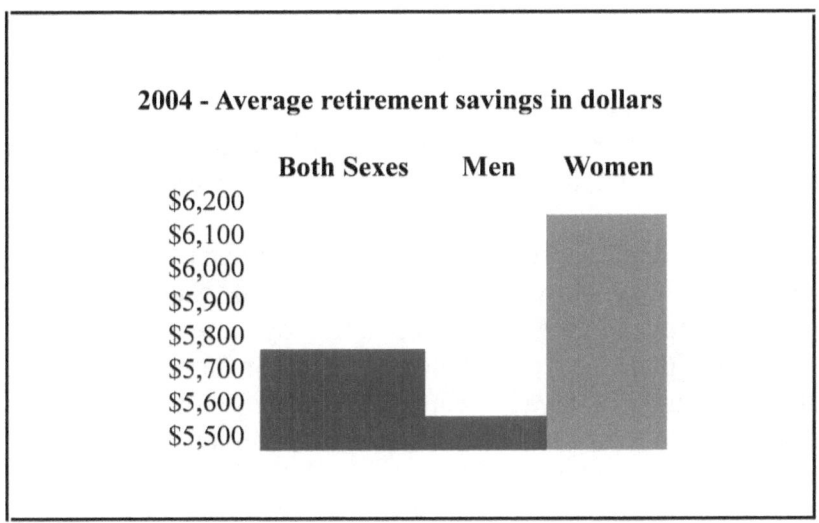

2004 - Average retirement savings in dollars

Source: Canada's Retirement Income Programs, 1997 to 2005
           Published by Statistics Canada, 2006

Notes: i. Data taken from the $40-$59.9k income group.
           ii. Includes year 2004 tax filers aged 25-64.
           iii. Savings refer to RRSP contributions and Pension
               Adjustment (PA) as reported in the 2004 tax year.
               The PA is used to estimate retirement savings
               through (other) Registered Pension Plans (RPPs).
           iv. The number of tax filers who saved: Men - 1.28m; Women - 1.04m
           v. Men are putting 47% of their savings in RRSPs.
           vi. Women are putting 41.5% of their savings into RRSPs.
           vii. Men are putting 53% of their savings into RPPs.
           viii. Women are putting 58.5% of their savings into RPPs.

Charts & Spreadsheets

Chart # 12

Chart # 12 is an interesting graph and I thought that its inclusion might be beneficial to many people.

The information provided is essentially about when we retire.

It states that during the 80's, Canadians were retiring after their 63rd birthday.

Meanwhile, during the late 90's Canadians were retiring before their 61st birthday. However, after the year 2002 the trend shifted and Canadians stayed in the workplace until they were older.

The interesting comment here is that it states, "Exerts predict that increasingly in the 21st century, Canadians will need to continue to work well into their retirement years to supplement their pension.

PLAN YOUR RETIREMENT-DON'T OUTLIVE YOUR MONEY!/ KITE   CHART # 12

MEDIAN RETIREMENT AGE GRAPH   MEDIAN RETIREMENT AGE

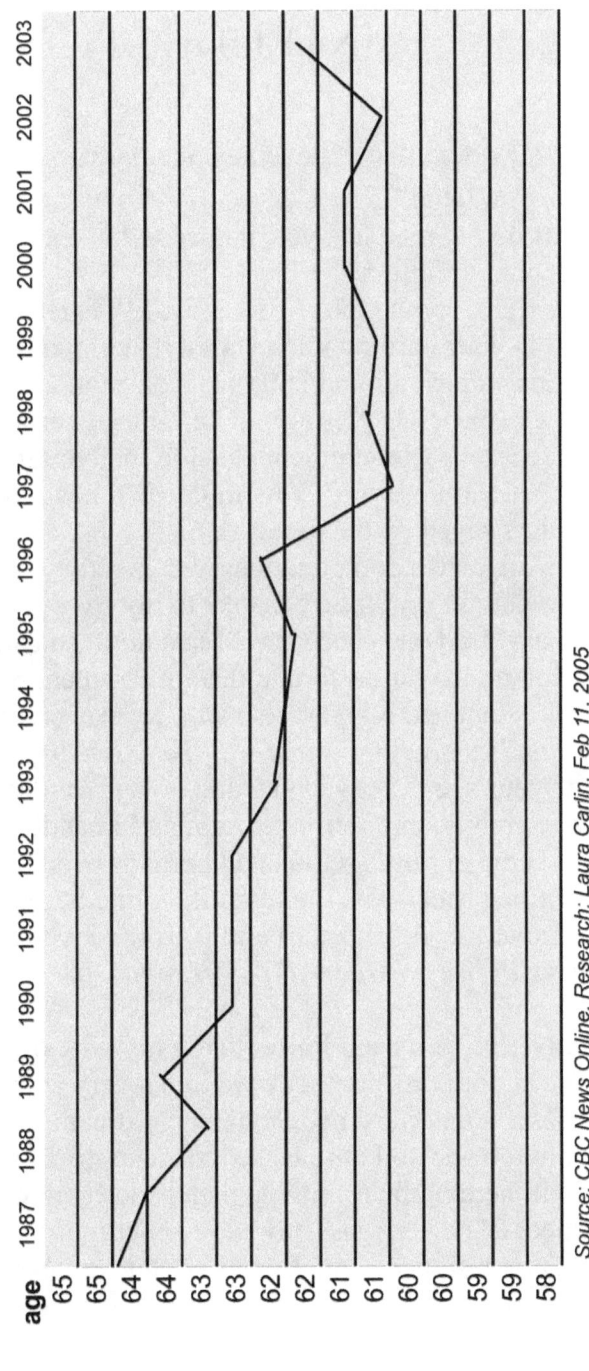

Source: CBC News Online. Research: Laura Carlin, Feb 11, 2005

NOTES: i.   During the late 80s it can be seen that Canadians were retiring after their 63rd birthday.
ii.   During the late 90s Canadians were retiring before their 61st birthday.
iii. As the graph shows, the trend shifts after 2002, showing that Canadians remain in the workplace until they are older.
iv.   Experts predict that, increasingly in the 21st century, Canadians will need to continue to work well into their retirement years to supplement their pension
v.   An early start on preparing your Retirement Plan can result in your owning a sizeable nest egg when you are in your sixties.
      This could enable you to leave the workplace earlier and, unlike others, live in financial freedom.

INTRODUCTION

So you would like to have an annual income of around $60,000 when you retire?

Sounds o.k. to me. But you'll need to have about $1,500,000 in your bank account to fund it.

That's right, about ONE MILLION, FIVE-HUNDRED THOUSAND Dollars earning interest of 4% will likely provide you with that sort of money, around $60,000 each year.

Quite a respectable pension you might say, especially when added to any federal or government pension that you may qualify for.

"But that's impossible!" you argue. "I'll never have a million and a half dollars saved by the time I'm 65."

Well, you have a point and that was exactly what I said when I was forty. But now in my sixties, thanks to my easy plan I am rich, so buy the book and read on - because if I can do it, so can you.

You can no longer be certain that government pensions will fund your retirement needs and worse still, reports predict that in future years, *three families on every street will likely live in poverty*!

But if your age is between 25 and 50 and you're pretty well sure that you can exercise some self-constraint and in addition, make an effort to save some of your income and perhaps even take on a part time job if deemed necessary, then you'll be fine because this book has a *proven* plan that's easy but smart and it worked well for Polly and me. *If you have desire and the will power to last the distance it could work well for you too.*

Twenty-five years ago Polly (that's my wife of over 40 years) and I had almost nothing. Yet today we live a very comfortable retirement lifestyle that most people can only dream of. I want you to live that dream too and so I am pleased to share my plan with you and you'll find it all here in the following pages - user friendly and no strings attached. It's a very easy-to-read format too. I also include some of my personally designed spreadsheets so that you can project your future savings with ease. Believe me, you'll never have another opportunity like this one. As the future years roll by you'll just love watching your money-tree grow, just like I did.

Remember, we don't often regret the things we DO do. It's usually the things we *don't* do that we regret and when you realize that on average, *2 out of every 3 families living on your street are unprepared for retirement,* you have to believe that there are going to be millions of regrets very soon. World wide the figures may be much worse and only you know if you are going to be one of those statistics who is destined to live their retirement in poverty.

When it comes to personal finance and the immense wealth that can be accumulated by a small but regular input of savings contributions, most Canadians are very naïve. *I believe that in Canada, every high school curriculum should include Personal Financial Management 101. If people learned at a young age how to properly manage debt and credit, everyone, especially students would have the knowledge and incentive to build a decent pension for themselves.*

There are many financial institutions all across the nation that are associated with major grocery supermarkets. What is wrong with adding an extra dollar or two to your pension fund at the check out every time you grocery shop? Two dollars saved, a couple of times each week wouldn't buy you an executive jet, but it would be a start to building a decent retirement fund for yourself. And as you approached retirement you would see how much you would have saved without realizing it. You might even be encouraged to add each week an extra twenty or thirty dollars. Practice that habit for ten or so years and likely old age destitution would give you a miss.

Yes. There's a major tragedy lurking out there.

But it needn't be like that for you. This is your opportunity and maybe your LAST opportunity to feather your nest for that retirement that you want. So come with me as I take you through these pages. Jump on, hold tight and enjoy the ride. I think that this is a trip that you will not regret taking.

Let me say here, that I am immediately encouraged by your intentions to stay with me. But be careful - I have heard it said that the road to hell is paved with good intentions. Stay the course and success will be yours to enjoy. You will be the envy of all your friends, because while they will be spending their winters at home, you'll be cruising the seven seas or jetting off to exotic places. A retirement to dream of, and your dreams will be a reality just like mine are.

Most of us think that we have the right to enjoy a secure and comfortable retirement in our later years and people look forward to this phase of their life with enthusiasm. In fact, if they had the opportunity, many people still in full time employment, would happily trade in their present working life for a stress-free retirement in the sun right now.

DREAMING OR PLANNING? – Which group are you in?

When it comes to actually *planning* for retirement, most of you are left at the starting gate. You just don't know how to go about it and actually, you are in the majority. You think about retirement from time to time and even discuss it with friends. You hope that your retirement will be carefree and comfortable. But in truth, your retirement years rely mainly on hopes and dreams. (Does this sound familiar?) You do not have any clearly defined plans, cost assessments or an investment strategy that could help you reach your goal. Mostly, people like this are too busy enjoying their life during their working years, and they can only think along the lines of, "Why save for tomorrow? We could all be dead by then."

People in this group could probably afford to have a marvellous retirement, but rather than prudently put away money each month for themselves, they foolishly spend it on others or for unnecessary treats that they want and I stress the word *unnecessary*.

This lackadaisical approach to a happy retirement is unwise and the people in this first group are progressing along a road that can almost surely lead to disaster and major disappointment.

But there is the other group. These smart people realize quite early in their adult life, that they need to seriously *plan* for the retirement that they really want. They will need to save sufficient money to afford the lifestyle they seek and to take care of their future personal needs, especially when they are too old to look after themselves. They carefully assess the cost, deny themselves some pleasures along the way, and regularly put aside measured amounts of savings to finance the plan. The result is that at some point later in their life, usually in their fifties or sixties, they find themselves in the happy position of being debt free and the owners of a significant nest-egg. They are able to give up full-time employment and start to live out their dream.

Now is the time to ask yourself, "Which group am I with?"

Let's find out.

Do you have a clear picture of what your retirement will be like and if it will really be achievable?

Have you assessed the cost with a reasonable degree of accuracy?

Do you deny yourself pleasures today in the knowledge that any money put aside now will have a major positive impact on your money tree?

Do you have a strategic plan that together with financial projections will get you where you want to be?

Have you explored new ideas such as paying down your mortgage early, thereby creating added savings for your nest egg?

Are you making regular contributions to a long-term financial plan?

Do you have a set of financial charts and grids to work with so that you can make accurate predictions for your Retirement Plan?

If you can answer yes to most of these questions then you have a very good chance of achieving your goal. If however you are like most people – and I was – you belong with the group of people who need to act NOW or you won't be able to retire with a comfortable standard of living. You will likely need to remain in full-time employment throughout your life so as to continue with your monthly payments. Clearly, your retirement plan is unprepared and full of vague expectations. You may have a handful of R.R.S.P.'s and the hope of a pension. You might even have a three or four-bedroom house that you intend to use as the cornerstone to finance your retirement.

If this person is really you then you are making a dangerous mistake and you need to make some serious changes NOW! But read on. I'll show you why and I'll show you how.

THE ROAD MAP – You won't get to your retirement dream without one.

As you work your way through the various chapters of this book you will see regular references to the phrase, "If you don't know where you are going then any road will get you there." This is not some witty play on words but rather a serious reminder that setting out on an uncharted course will take you somewhere, but most likely, *not* where you had in mind.

If you intend to arrive at a particular destination, you must first know where you are and then know exactly where you want to be. Further, if you have studied the entire route in detail and are aware of any difficulties you may encounter en route, you will always have a good chance of arriving *safely* at your chosen destination.

Of course, there will likely be hidden dangers along the way lurking for the unwary and so to avoid the pitfalls you must be constantly on the lookout and regularly refer to your plan while confirming your position. The same goes for almost everything that you want and a successful retirement plan is nothing to be casual about. So get serious – plan your dream, cost it out, decide how to achieve the funds needed to cover the costs, exercise self-restraint during your working years and you will have an excellent chance to see all those dreams come true.

This book will provide you with a retirement plan and many of the answers that you are probably seeking. But to see your dream come true you need to start working on it NOW. (I've said it again).

WOMEN – A major influence in future retirement statistics

If you are a woman and in particular, one of the baby boomers born during the middle years of the 20th century, you likely already know that you are expected to greatly influence what retirement will be like in the future. This is due in part to the major increase in the number of women who will be receiving a company pension. Also, women will see their own retirement as an opportunity to do more than merely cease full-time employment.

We are also told that with each passing year more seniors are finding that the income from their pensions is insufficient to cover their monthly living costs even to the point that more of them are finding it necessary to visit food banks.

IGNORE THE PLAN – A Dangerous Mistake

Without wishing to sound too repetitive, may I strongly recommend that if you have not done so before, you now think seriously about your future retirement years and how you intend to finance them. Perhaps begin by first discussing the implications with the members of your immediate family because in some way they will all be effected.

Next, you will need to decide on how to take appropriate action. You can do this with the aid of the schemes described in this book and by preparing some definite plans to get yourself where you want to be when you are around 65 years young. If you follow this suggestion and can put the plans into action and thereby become fully committed to this life-long project, then everything should work out just fine for you. Moreover, by taking the time needed to thoroughly prepare your Retirement Plan you will have a clear idea as to how your future will evolve and what to expect. You will be in control.

To procrastinate is folly and while there may never be a *perfect* time that you feel is right for you to start, you really have no choice. The years will just fly by and suddenly you wake up one morning and discover that you are in your sixties and are still thinking that one day you will start saving towards your retirement. Then it will be too late. But don't worry - you probably won't be alone! We are told that most Canadians will not have a retirement in the style that we have come to know it.

Remember, you can't go back, and it really is later than you may think. So… better start today.

Preparing and maintaining a properly written retirement plan may appear daunting but really, it is not as difficult as it sounds. Just be willing to take the time and trouble to create one that fits your particular needs and you will discover, as I did, the huge benefits that will be waiting for you and for those you love in your golden years.

Also, (and this is really the big buzz) you will experience an enormous sense of excitement while your plan is actually in progress. Just imagine, as the years roll past you'll find yourself becoming quite affluent on paper, especially in the later years. As if by magic, you will watch your plan unfold just as you had projected and on one especially exciting moment, you will realize that your retirement dreams are actually going to materialise. Yes! Your years of hard work and self-constraint really are going to bear fruit. Big buzz - big time!

Another huge bonus along the way will be the *peace of mind* you will experience, when, as you regularly review your savings, you realize that your plan is progressing perfectly and the targets are all being achieved thanks mainly to your prudent investments and your informed decisions. The contents of *Robert Kite's Successful Retirement Plan* will help you by showing you how to make those decisions. It may also help you by alerting you to the opportunities that many others are missing mainly as a result of stubbornness, pride or ignorance.

For example, thousands of people are not drawing pension benefits. Ms. Denise Savoie, Member of Parliament for Victoria, British Columbia addressed the Canadian House of Commons in Ottawa on March 19, 2007. She stated, "*Large numbers of people are eligible but are not receiving benefits. According to Statistics Canada right now there are 130,000 low-income seniors who are eligible for the GIS (government income supplement) but are not receiving it. Eighty per cent of those missing out on the GIS are women, most of whom are very elderly. There are also about 55,000 who are missing out on CPP (Canadian Pension Plan) retirement benefits.*" By reading and learning of this possible oversight by others, it is hoped that you will become wiser and more astute so as to claim all that you are entitled to.

Throughout the several years of your Retirement Plan, you and your family will be delighted to watch your investments and savings grow to almost the precise values that you projected. You will feel justly proud. And justly rich!

DISCOVERING MY OVERSIGHT – Just in Time

The adventure began for me one evening when I was in my forties. Polly and I were spending a happy evening with some old friends, Roy and Joan – old in the sense that we had known them for quite a few years. In fact, they were about our own age. We had been to a favourite restaurant and returned to their apartment for a coffee and a nightcap before heading home.

During the evening, Roy and I got around to discussing our future years and in particular, retirement. After all, we were in mid-life but the years had been flying by while all of us had been enjoying the good times. We seriously wanted those halcyon days to continue forever, even on a pension.

"So what type of Retirement Plan do you have, Robert?" Roy poured us a brandy and relaxed into his armchair.

Roy and Joan were both employed at a local college where Joan worked as a senior administrator and Roy lectured in computer technology. He obviously knew his stuff and he always seemed to have something to say about finances too.

The four of us used to talk a lot about our respective futures and our efforts at savings and investments. I remember, on one occasion we all laughed when Roy admitted that he stayed up half the night studying the financial pages of the daily papers. Fortunately, his lectures didn't start until late morning.

I usually felt quite comfortable with what Roy said about money-related issues and, as my job included long-term financial planning, he used to enjoy throwing difficult questions in my direction to try to catch me but it was all done in good humour.

Polly and I enjoyed their company a great deal, to the point that it was with Roy that I'd put some savings into a Swiss bank account. We'd hoped that the value of our investment would grow through the increased strength of the Swiss franc, and it did! But that's a story for another time.

I tried to think of an answer to Roy's question. He'd caught me off guard this time because I realized that I didn't have a formal retirement plan as such – I had always thought that I was too young. In a sense I had a plan, but it was in my head and certainly nothing tangible on paper that demonstrated a route to my anticipated goal. But now I was being made acutely aware that in fact I had no plan, not in a formal sense at least and I felt embarrassed that I'd been found out neglecting such an important issue. It wasn't exactly a life-threatening oversight but it suddenly became clear that at some point in my future life it could be a huge disadvantage not to have a well thought-out Retirement Plan and by then, well, it would all be too late. I would not be able to go back in time. I would only have regrets.

"My Retirement Plan is essentially financial, Roy." I hedged, unsure where the conversation was going. "What I mean to say is... that my plan is financially driven and as a result, the rest of it falls into place." I felt o.k. with my quickly fabricated response.

"That sounds good," replied Roy. "Your investments are well diversified, then?"

"Oh yes, of course." That wasn't really the case, either. "Are you well diversified too, Roy?"

"You need to be, Robert," he answered, "so that if anything goes wrong in one sector of the market, you have a good chance of being well protected by the other sectors."

"That's right," I said. "Not putting all your eggs in one basket." I was pleased that the expression had come to mind.

"Exactly," Roy agreed.

PREPARING MY PLAN –A Retirement Dream on Paper

I remember that I was anxious to get a few things down on paper and so the next weekend, I took one of my long-term financial plans that I used in business and modified it, until it was appropriately adapted for my personal needs so as to at least have a starting point. During the next few weeks I spent most of my time shaping and re-shaping my plan. The objective was that Polly and I would have sufficient savings and income together with our state pensions so as to be able to afford a comfortable retirement and do the things that we wanted to do. I followed the same style of strategy that I had developed for my business plans as part of my daily job. Establishing my present position, projected a reasonably accurate long-term financial forecast and connected the dots between the two points.

I've always been grateful for Roy's wake-up call and the fact that I didn't leave it any longer. I was in my forties at the time. Later in this book you'll discover that if you don't already have a Retirement Plan it's important for you to start on it immediately no matter what your age; in fact the younger the better as it gives more time for your money-tree to grow. I will show you the immense power of compounding.

Now Polly and I are in our mature years, we somewhat resemble those two people you see in the investment ads on the TV commercials – the couple with white hair and togetherness, each wearing a sweater over an expensive tan – debt free with the luxury home and fancy car. But remember, it hasn't always been this way.

Twenty or so short years ago I had little or no savings whatsoever. Yes, I'd always had a steady job, in fact one that paid very well and certainly, we'd always had some equity in our home and maybe a few thousand dollars saved and sheltered within a Canadian R. R. S. P. portfolio, but like most of our friends, we'd always had whatever we wanted with little regard to the cost or how or when we'd get to pay for it. We used to laugh as we said, "Mr. VISA will buy it for us!" How foolish we were.

We gave no thought to the urgency or to the wisdom of saving money for our retirement. I suppose, like everyone else, I had assumed that a good job and a large paycheque would always be there, after all, it always had. And so, while we were busy loving our life and each other, enjoying trips abroad and buying bigger houses, we didn't realize how quickly the years were passing and the opportunity to prepare sensibly for our retirement was passing us by.

Then one early morning, while I was getting ready to go to work, I was looking in the mirror while shaving and noticed just how much my hair had started to turn white. I remembered the conversation I'd had with Roy and realized then, once and for all that the years were beginning to race by. Polly and I had also started to put on a little weight and we no longer stayed up at nights to watch the late show. Yes, these were little signals that the years were definitely catching up with us and that old age was heading in our direction, fast.

And now, years later, our current home is a mortgage-free luxury condo in a respectable part of town and we can live comfortably on our pensions. In addition, we have substantial R. R. S. P. holdings, some savings funds, a portfolio of investments, an assortment of shares and substantial deposit account balances. In addition, we recently sold our delightful little condo in Spain for cash!

"Not bad," I tell my mirror every day. In fact, nearly every morning when I wake up, within a few seconds or so, I think of our wonderful life and a large grin spreads from ear to ear.

GRAB THE BRASS RING – Planning can work for you

I have written this book because the retirement plan that I wrote for myself worked. I believe it can work for almost anybody, given the right conditions. A little bit of luck helps too but overall, if you make a detailed plan and stick to it, you have a very good chance of enjoying a happy retirement just like Polly and I do. I want you to learn from our experience and benefit from our great success and I offer you that chance now. So go ahead, grab the brass ring and watch your money-tree grow just as we did.

Many of us, both men and women – in fact, especially women – when we are in our forties or fifties, suddenly realize that our senior years are approaching much faster than we thought possible and there is nothing we can do about it but accept it. The changes that take place in our appearance can worry some of us and so can the change in pace. We slow down while things around us seem to speed up. Sometimes we even walk into a room and wonder why we're there! Well, don't worry, I'm told that it's just part of the process.

EFFECTIVE FINANCIAL PLANNING –The Key

As we near the golden years, we realize that good health is going to be vital to a happy retirement, and if we stop smoking, eat sensibly and exercise regularly then the rest, as they say, is in the lap of the Gods. No. There is not a lot we can do about assuring ourselves of good health.

The other thing that is going to be vital to a happy retirement is of course money. It's a worry if you have lots of it and have to keep it invested with minimal risk. But it's an even bigger worry if you don't have enough – especially when you get older and you hear that your employer is considering replacing you because you're either too expensive or too slow.

There are benefits to having a Retirement Plan in place at any time in your life but make no mistake about it, the sooner the better.

The worries about money that the approaching senior years can bring-on are replaced by the pleasure that you experience when you track your Retirement Plan and see your security nest-egg grow as the years slip by. With your retirement on the horizon and your Retirement Plan coming to fruition, your financial hopes are in fact becoming a reality and they will provide you with the happy retirement years that you want so much. Retirement will be your years to enjoy but remember, the main key to this future lifestyle is Effective Financial Planning. But you must start NOW! (I've said it again).

I respectfully invite you to continue reading through this book and to learn from it as you develop the confidence that will come with knowledge. You will discover how to harness and use the power that comes from having accurate financial information and you will quickly gain whatever knowledge I can share from my own life's business experience.

Remember, unless you have an unexpected windfall, (and you may do) a successful and happy retirement will only be possible for you if you do some serious preparation and make some hard decisions. Self-constraint will definitely be the name of the game – there is no magic formula. You will be accountable for your own destiny and I caution you now, do not depend on any unexpected massive windfall.

Neither is this a circus. I cannot provide you with tricks to create large savings accounts or valuable assets overnight. I am not a financial wizard, I am not an investment consultant, and I certainly cannot make any promises to you except perhaps for one. If you choose NOT to plan for your retirement and to ignore all of the warnings that we hear about pensions that are increasingly under threat, then the chances of you having a happy, carefree retirement will be very slim indeed. It simply will not happen and I can promise you that you will be heading for a senior's life in dire destitution.

What I will do throughout this book is reveal to you the plan that worked for me, my personal successful Retirement Plan. I will tell you of the things I learned over the years and the ideas that I was able to put to good and effective use both in my work and in our personal lives. You will find that I will repeat, probably quite often, some sentences that I feel you need to digest thoroughly. Forgive me for this but I believe that it is necessary to get you to focus your attention on the points that are paramount to make your plan successful. As I see it, my job here is to encourage you succeed and avoid failure at all costs. If repetition is needed to drive the point home then I apologise, but so be it.

I hope these various pages will show you what you need to know so as to be able to successfully prepare and manage a Retirement Plan that will really work for your future. A personal plan, tailored by you, for you, that will guide you to the financial security you want so much.

I will show you the many financial charts and grids that I used to benefit Polly and me. Charts like the ones I devised and used successfully for some of the world's largest institutions. I will show you how our personal funds grew over a period of less than twenty-five years to the level where we can now enjoy a retirement life free from any money worries whatsoever.

I will include many hints, tips and suggestions that I've learned during forty years of listening to experts. As some of these same guiding principles are still being voiced by many of today's journalists and broadcasters, I think we can safely assume that they have stood the test of time.

I know that this book will not be a classic and that there will likely be no Pulitzer Prize coming my way, but if I can help you to make some informed decisions, to learn how to exercise self-discipline now and as a result, have a secure and happy retirement in later years, then my aim will be achieved.

Remember, your plan can be quite flexible up to a point, but preparing for the long term means that you must necessarily avoid making too many or too frequent changes. Seek professional advice, consider your options, make informed decisions and then stick to your guns and you will likely succeed in your objective.

Whatever you do with your savings and investments remember this. There are many sensible tips and sayings but if I had to name just a few for you to focus on, particularly with regard to mutual investments they would be these.

Usually, the higher the return you receive for your investment the greater the risk. Stay with a level of risk that you feel entirely comfortable with.

Diversify your investments. Do not put all of your eggs in the same basket. Spreading your savings or investments over a range of sectors is spreading the level of risk and this is a smart thing to do.

If the rate of return is so high for an investment fund that it appears too good to be true, let your instinct be your guide.

What goes up can always come down. Avoid greed at all costs.

Remember that there is a difference between investing and gambling. Make sure that you understand which of the two you are doing.

During the Fall of 2006, the Government of Canada announced a change in the taxing of Investment Trusts. This resulted in having a major impact on the market values of these types of funds. Many people lost thousands of dollars on paper overnight which was especially distressing for retired seniors who saw the value of their pension plans reduced considerably.

Anyone who sold their Investment Trust funds immediately would have cashed in the paper losses. Fortunately, most investors were diversified and so the losses were contained and minimized. However, my friend Joe thought that the Investment Trusts were so good that he invested ninety percent of his retirement savings in them. I understand that his paper losses exceeded forty thousand dollars overnight. Poor Joe. He did not diversify and he paid the price.

But enough of the bad news – this is a good news book because the pages are full of positive information and the fact that you are reading it, leads me to believe that you will prepare an effective Retirement Plan for yourself and live to enjoy your retirement dream.

I hope that you take pleasure from the read and more importantly, that you will prepare a successful Retirement Plan so as to provide yourself with the future lifestyle you deserve. Good luck to you!

Chapter one
GETTING STARTED
What do I need to know?

Retirement is an experience that we all hope to enjoy, although as young adults we probably don't give it much thought. And why should we? After all, retirement is really for older people such as our parents or grandparents. Well, yes. But let's think about it for a moment. You may be a grandparent yourself one day and even if you think of that situation as an unlikely prospect, you can certainly hope to arrive at the age of retirement and when you do, be happy in the knowledge that you can afford the luxury of doing just whatever you want to do and whenever you want to do it.

Believe it or not, when I was a child I thought that old people were born that way. My immature mind wouldn't allow me to think that these grey haired, bent over people were children many years previously and that perhaps one day (if I was lucky) I would look like them. Well, was I in for a big surprise when I discovered the truth and that in fact, my youth would fade and my skin would wrinkle and any savings I had in the bank looked miniscule compared with the size of my retirement expectations. Yes, the retirement years, those years of looking older, are there for all of you unless something drastic happens, and depending on how much planning has been done, the experience will be either very pleasant or something else. My advice to you from my present vantage point is

DON'T LET IT BE SOMETHING ELSE!

Recently, I was telling a great-nephew about retirement when he asked, "Uncle Robert, If we are expected to work all our adult lives, why shouldn't we all have fun and play when we get to fifty?"

I was a little surprised at such a question coming from a young lad and frankly, one that I had to think about before I could provide a sensible answer. I told him that unless you're rich or have wealthy parents you'd better get a good education and a well-paying job. You would also need to start saving some of your income otherwise you would have no chance to play in your later years.

THE RULES OF THE GAME – Follow the rules and you could win big!

I'm writing this book with the thought that you're a bit like I was when I was in my thirties, forties or fifties – a little ambitious, wanting to live well and have some expensive toys, travel, and buy the things that you want now rather than later. Then, at some point in the future, retire and enjoy many years of playing in the sun with those you love.

If you fit within that age group (or even younger) perhaps you'd like to take a moment to think about that. Take a look around you or if you like, visualize some of your own family members, the older ones in particular. Can you clearly define in your mind how they're managing their retirement?

Do you envy them? Are they active and perhaps even more important, are they doing what they want to do in their retirement? Do they have sufficient savings invested to provide them with some creature comforts? Can they afford to have some fun and be happy after having worked hard all their lives, probably making lots of money for someone else?

Actually, these are some of the questions that you should be asking yourself. But there is an even bigger question that you need to ask yourself. Would you be content or even happy if, in your future years you were spending your own retirement doing precisely what they're doing? Be honest with yourself.

Well, whatever the answer is, you should know that you might easily end up with that particular retirement lifestyle, the one you gave in your answer, whether you want it or not.

The rule of this game is very simple: *The earlier in life you can decide that a comfortable retirement is for you, the more likely it will be possible.*

Do not procrastinate. Start to save for your retirement - NOW! I did and I don't regret it.

WHAT DO YOU MEAN BY RETIREMENT?

Different people have different meanings for the word *retirement*. Generally, most people see retirement as finishing their working days entirely, and together with a spouse or a partner, enjoying their time actively involved in leisurely pursuits such as travelling, golf, tennis, sailing or some other activity. Of course, for this preferred lifestyle you need to be financially independent throughout your several retirement years. And yes, you may want to have enough left over so that you can provide a worthwhile legacy for your family so as to give them a helping hand in their young life.

Other people see retirement as an opportunity to be active in volunteer work and there are a variety of jobs that can provide meaningful employment and great satisfaction for those interested in that. But as with the earlier option, with this lifestyle you also need to be able to finance yourself.

Then again, some other people look forward to a retirement where they have a part time job that provides them with some income but without the major responsibilities that they carried in their full time employment. The money earned from part time work helps retirees to supplement any pension that they may receive and the activity and staff interaction helps them to remain alert and agile.

There are many other forms of retirement that people might have in mind too but generally, when you talk of retirement, you probably think of the first group, those people who choose to happily enjoy themselves with a leisurely pursuit, especially if you are still employed full time and do the commute grind to work every day. During our working years most of us can only think of retirement as being a life of doing nothing except playing our favourite activity, travelling and visiting family members. Sounds good doesn't it?

If this is you, then you should know that the Canadian or Quebec Pension Plan alone will *not* provide you with that aspired lifestyle, particularly if you have major debts such as a mortgage or car payments. You will definitely need to have other forms of income and of that, there is no doubt. However, you sensibly have selected this book to study and guide your retirement planning actions and so you have a very good chance of learning how to provide yourself with the retirement of your dreams. As I have said earlier, my simple retirement plan worked successfully for Polly and me and it can work for you too.

Anyone who begins saving for their retirement at fifteen years of age and makes regular financial contributions into their plan, no matter how small, is almost guaranteed a financially secure retirement, especially if the saved money remains untouched and is allowed to grow and benefit from the power of compounding. But if you are in your forties or fifties and do not currently have a Retirement Plan and have no intention of starting one, then the chances are almost inevitable that there will be NO retirement for you. You will need to make arrangements for a full time job or several part time ones to pay for your senior days. *A federal retirement pension alone will not be sufficient to sustain you.*

IMPORTANT POINT

AS A RESULT OF NOT HAVING ANY PERSONAL RETIREMENT PLAN,
RETIREMENT AS WE UNDERSTAND IT WILL NO LONGER EXIST FOR THOUSANDS, IF NOT MILLIONS, OF CANADIANS.

However, you may just feel that this book may provide you with some workable answers. I am enormously passionate about what my successful Retirement Plan has done for Polly and me and the enthusiasm in my writing style may just motivate you to start saving and so remove the grey clouds from your future years. I hope so anyway.

YOUR RETIREMENT NEST EGG - You have enough of It - but you're not saving it.

I remember very well the days when I had no retirement plan. We'd visit Montreal for a week at Christmas. Then we'd go to

Vancouver in March for a week. Later in the year we'd travel to England to see my sister and her husband and children. Then, in the late summer, we'd take a long weekend and drive down to Maryland to visit our friends Mary and Kevin and their family, our former neighbours in Toronto. You see, between us, Polly and I had enough money to afford a brilliant retirement financial plan but we were so naïve. *We were spending it as quickly as we were earning it.*

I remember in particular when one weekend we were visiting Kevin and Mary, the wives decided to go shopping in Washington and Kevin took his two boys and me fishing in his boat on Chesapeake Bay.

"How's life treating you in Canada?" Kevin asked as he swung his rod into a cast. The line sang a high-pitched zing as it sped through the loops. He knew Ontario well because he'd lived there for a number of years before heading south of the border.

"Pretty good, " I answered. "We seem to have everything we want. Robert junior is doing well at school and Polly seems very happy although she misses England terribly."

"How so?" asked Kevin, a former Brit himself.

"Well, you know how it is when you move across the world, Kevin. Sometimes, there's a tendency to cling to the past. Polly misses familiar places to visit and short drives to quaint villages. But on the whole, we don't do too badly."

"Badly?" Kevin raised his voice above the freshening wind. "Mary and I think you two do *bloody* well."

At the time I was surprised to hear him say that because I thought that we were living just an ordinary sort of life. But I suppose he was right. After all, we had a nice house in a reasonable part of town, three or four vacations each year, closets full of clothes, and as for shirts, well that was always my weakness as was Polly's for shoes. Still is, as a matter of fact.

The point I'm trying to make is that we really did have a lot and the money that we thought that we never had to save for retirement was in fact really there. But instead of putting it away and allowing it to grow like a plant for the later years in our lives when we would need a large nest egg, we were spending it on all sorts of things that we didn't really need – including interest payments on credit cards and a huge mortgage that we could have reduced if we had thought about it. But we didn't. We just didn't think!

Robert junior liked sports and art so there were some costs there for him, but not a lot. Whatever we wanted, we seemed to just go out and buy. Almost everything, except a retirement plan. How stupid we were. It simply never occurred to us that one day we would be old enough to retire and there would be a major cost if we wanted to continue our lifestyle but give up full time work. If anyone would even hire us full time when we were in our sixties. Worse still, as I was the main breadwinner, what would happen if I became seriously sick? Would the long-term disability insurance be enough to provide us with the lifestyle we had grown accustomed to? I doubt it. Yes. We were stupid alright.

YOUR OPPORTUNITY IS HERE – Have you recognized it yet?

Now back to our friends who actually *do* have a retirement plan. They're the sensible ones and if you happen to be one of them then I imagine that you have been very busy for quite some years, stuffing money into investment funds, bonds, cash and other forms of savings, so as to generate the right amounts of money to provide you with that wonderful lifestyle when you get there. Part-time work for you in retirement will not be compulsory, merely an option, because financially, you probably won't need it.

The several years leading up to retirement can be very interesting because as you come through your thirties and get used to being out of your twenties, you are suddenly faced with the shock realizing that next year you will be forty! For many people this can be a bit of a jolt, but it is only temporary and so you soldier on into and through your forties, armed with the confidence that life's experiences can provide.

Now that the forties are almost behind you, you start to find things changing a bit, about your person. Your hair for example. The colour doesn't seem as vibrant as it used to be and, wait a minute, isn't it getting a bit thinner on top?

"And now look," you say to yourself. "Next year I am going to be fifty. A half a century!"

And you get pains in your body everyday. Not big ones but little pains like muscle pains, and yet you didn't do anything strenuous yesterday. Last week it was your shoulder. This week it is your back.

"Where will it be next?" you ask yourself.

You wonder how others have coped with this event and when you look at your parents, you momentarily visualise yourself walking in their shoes. And you are only just fifty!

During the few years that follow you shrug it off but notice changes in your parents' behaviour too, and now start to think that the roles are being reversed – that they are fast becoming the children, and that you are becoming the parent of them. Yes. The future is here and the changes are many and you don't like the fact that they are happening fast.

The years themselves seem to speed up and the passage of time is racing at an alarming rate. You are now in your late fifties and your appearance is very different. The way you looked twenty years ago bothered you then, but now you wish you could go back to looking just that way. "After all," you tell yourself. "I looked quite good for my age and I never seemed to have any problem attracting the attention from the opposite sex."

Welcome to the sixties! Now you notice that your skin on your arms is wrinkling and you seem to be going to more funerals than ever before. "Oh my!" "Is this what old age is all about?"

Pretty well. But wait a minute. Just imagine life like that but without any nest egg. Imagine not having sufficient money in your savings accounts to afford an occasional vacation or a trip to a beauty parlour. Or how about a new set of golf clubs or perhaps a bigger boat to perk you up or a new car?

"No. The *impoverished* life as a senior is definitely not for me." That's what I told myself when I was in my forties and I hope that you are now of the same opinion. Remember, I speak from experience and have travelled the road to my late sixties. As Paul Anka wrote as a lyric, "I did it my way" and personally speaking as Robert Kite, I'm glad I did.

Now that you've been looking at the future through my eyes so to speak, I want to direct you back to *your* future. And so, in the years leading up to your retirement, be prepared for a small jolt. Your employer might just be one of those managers who will imagine that your white hair indicates that you're past your "best-before" or "sell by" date and that you are now too slow to grasp the complete picture.

Hopefully, when that time comes you will have sufficient funds in your savings accounts to provide you with an easy feeling of self-assurance and you will already know that a comfortable retirement will be there waiting for you.

But it will take a continuing amount of careful planning and regular monitoring of your money tree to ensure that your objective is constantly well focused and that your plan is on track. You want to be sure that the size of your nest egg is increasing in value and relatively close to the predictions you made when you first prepared your Retirement Plan.

You will know that most individual retirement experiences will vary considerably and as I said earlier, the actual ideas that you have about retirement today will likely change somewhat as time goes by.

Some seniors appear to have a wonderful life with enough money to do pretty well whatever they want. However, many pension experts are now reporting that if the current trend continues these types of people will be a vanishing breed.

Perhaps you have some friends or family members who enjoy this enviable lifestyle – the sort of folk who spend the winter in Florida, Mexico, California, or Arizona. The same people who enjoy their summers in Canada with the grandchildren and other members of their family, maybe at the cottage or by the lake. They play golf or tennis or maybe have a boat, they travel on international trips and go on ocean cruises, in fact, let's face it, they seem to have carved out for themselves the so-called "Good Life."

Then there are other seniors who don't seem to go away very much at all. This may be their choice of course, and no one can blame them if they want to just watch their money-tree grow, as it certainly will if during their retirement they have a substantial regular income and choose not to spend it.

On the other hand, their sedentary lifestyle may be due to a *lack* of available money and perhaps their entire regular monthly income is limited solely to the Canadian or the Quebec Pension Plan and the Old Age Security pension. If this were the case then unfortunately they would be severely restricted in what they could afford to do with their time.

It might be that during their working years they thought that the value in their house would be enough to provide a retirement fund but unfortunately for them, property prices dropped. Or perhaps they still have a big mortgage and interest rates have risen and they did not realize the costs involved in everyday living. There is certainly no shame in that but what a tragedy? Particularly if in their earlier years when they were working, they made good money and had the opportunity to save and plan for their old age but had no knowledge of how to go about it.

Did opportunity just pass them by? They had the chance that would have almost guaranteed them a comfortable retirement but for whatever the reason, they never had the ability or the motivation to get around to actually planning it and making it happen. Even today, many people believe that the federal pension will be enough for them to enjoy a decent retirement in their older years. And women are especially vulnerable. Statistics Canada reported in 2006 that large numbers of retired widows are forced to live in poverty due to a tragic miscalculation as to how they would be provided for in the event of their husband's death.

In many western countries including Canada and the United States, hundreds of retirees are becoming destitute, declaring bankruptcy because their company pension became swallowed up as the firm went to the wall.

I was taught at a very young age that before you can seize an opportunity you must first recognize it. Opportunities pass by people every day of their lives and they simply don't see them. And so I learned to look hard for opportunities, to seek them out and dare I say, you should do the same.

I am led to hope that you will see this book as *your* opportunity and recognize it for what it is, a chance to secure for yourself a happy and fulfilling, financially independent retirement. We did and you can too.

But back to the group who seem to have it all. Did they inherit a legacy or win the lottery or something? If not, then some people might say that they must have had a good plan to get them to where they are today. Pensions, RRSPs or something.

They probably saved, invested and listened. And you know what? In essence, that is all you need to do. But you must start NOW!

IMPORTANT POINT

THE THREE STEPS TO A SECURE RETIREMENT

~ SAVE, INVEST, BE VIGILANT ~

When you sit down and commence preparing your Retirement Plan you will need to clearly define your future expectations. This way you will know what your retirement goals are and the preparation of the Retirement Plan to reach those objectives will be made that much easier.

I have included charts and financial grids to help you do this. Also, as you work your way through your plan during the remaining working years, it is imperative that you regularly track your plan so that you personally have absolute knowledge as to where your savings are and what their precise value is. I cannot overstress the importance of this – it is paramount to your success. You can only trust yourself. You will discover why later in the book.

Of course, if you have mutual funds or company stock, it will be of no use if you check your local city indices where you live, in Vancouver or Halifax for example, if you don't know the sector of your particular basket of investments.

Imagine for just a moment that you have a large investment in precious metals, including gold, and as you drive home from work the news on your car radio tells you that the stock market rose ninety-five points this afternoon. After a busy and successful day this news immediately makes you feel pleased that your mutual funds too have probably had a good day. But in fact, although they were not mentioned in the newscast, gold-related funds actually had a bad day and dropped three percent of their morning value.

In truth, if you are well diversified you will have nothing too much to worry about. Just the same, if you check the websites or the evening newspapers you could learn of *all* the major news relating to precious metals including your personally owned gold stocks. Relying on just one medium such as the radio left you with only part of the story that you needed to know. If you become dedicated to learn *everything* about your money tree you will arm yourself with the all of the news and have a comprehensive understanding of the finer details of your portfolio.

IMPORTANT POINT

MAKE A HABIT OF REGULARLY CHECKING
YOUR INVESTMENT FUNDS
MONITOR THE SECTORS AND KNOW
THE DOLLAR VALUES

~ REMAIN IN CONTROL ~

Constant awareness at this level is not completely necessary of course but the point that I make here is that if you try to become attuned to learning all about your investments, then you have knowledge and that can be powerful indeed, especially when you make the annual trip to visit your financial advisor for example. You want to understand as much as possible about what he or she is telling you.

61

You will feel in control and you will feel good that you have all of the information that will enable you to develop and consider any options you think necessary. When you sit down with your fund manager you'll be able to speak their language with confidence and completely understand their strategy. You will be well prepared. You may even be one step ahead of them. *You* will be in control. And why not – it *is* your money!Ignorance is NOT bliss – you need to know everything you can about your investments. Your fund manager may not agree with this of course but the funds represent your hard earned money and you need it to grow as quickly as it can (with the least possible risk necessary) to underpin that retirement you dream of.

Earlier, I mentioned the importance of *tracking* your investments and this is another point that your fund manager may not agree with. They will tell you that this is their job and so you do not need to do this. In fact, they ask you not to look at your funds too regularly because you might tend to react unnecessarily when the values take a dip. Your telephone calls will interrupt their day.

My position is this. That regular monitoring of your investments is vital so that you know what is going on behind the scenes so to speak. I would agree that you should not overreact every time a drop in values takes place but personally, I feel more comfortable knowing what is going on with my money than if I did not.

IMPORTANT POINT

IF YOU KNOW WHERE YOU ARE GOING
THEN AT THE VERY LEAST
YOU WILL KNOW WHEN YOU HAVE ARRIVED THERE

I also think that monitoring the values of your investments is especially advisable if you are to achieve your objective, because if you just put your savings into what you perceive as a worthwhile investment and then just forget about it, all sorts of things can happen that you may not know about. Some of them good of course, but there could be many negative activities too and a fund manager has many clients to be concerned about and you are just one.

You want to be on the cutting edge of your investments particularly during your working years. The journey to retirement can be long and arduous and you need to be assessing if the growth of your money tree is anything like what you projected it to be. With the help of the plan you will always know how much you will need for your retirement and so to monitor the growth is important. At all times you want to be fully aware about everything in your savings funds, including the market trends.

You need to be acquainted with your funds so you can almost predict their movement within the marketplace. That's the optimum, and while it may sound a bit too complicated now, you'll be amazed what can happen if you apply yourself. You need to be interested and you need to be dedicated because after all, what is more interesting than watching your own money tree growing? Feeling yourself becoming rich can be fun!

What a shock it would be if you woke in the morning only to see a photo of your fund manager on the front page of the newspaper with a caption,

"FUND MANAGER DOES A RUNNER!"

Unlikely of course, but it has been known to happen and a regular watch over your funds might alert you if things start to act strangely.

In a perfect world, this money-saving mania should become a minor hobby so that you are right on top of your game with your Retirement Plan. If you follow this philosophy, imagine the immense knowledge you will have by the time you get to retirement. You might even want to write a book or conduct some lectures so that others may learn and benefit from your wealth of personal experience. Psychologically, (and financially) it might be very rewarding.

Tell yourself that this project is going to become the most important thing to occupy your mind. Naturally, there will be many distractions but overall, you must do whatever is necessary to remind yourself to review your *Monthly Living Cost* budget, your *Monthly Savings Growth* chart, your *Individual R.R.S.P. Funds* grid, your *Mortgage Payment Plan* and your overall *Retirement Plan*. Because that is what you should want to do if you are to achieve your objective. You need to keep your finger on the pulse to follow the four principals of knowledge.

i.   Know how much you have.

ii.   Know where it is.

iii.   Know what is happening to it.

iv.   Know what is likely to happen to it tomorrow.

If the value of your money tree is several millions of dollars then I suspect that you will choose not to monitor your savings too regularly. I would imagine that you have diversified and have sums of money with a few different banks. This way, a crooked fund manager would make you only a little less wealthy.

For the rest of us, things are different. A crooked fund manager would wipe us out. We would be destitute and grief stricken. So, notwithstanding <u>most fund managers are very honest and upright citizens</u>, keep your hand on your wallet, so to speak.

FUNDS MANAGERS – Can you judge a book by its cover?

I have some friends who are investment advisers. These are professional men and women. Most of them, when they were quite young knew exactly what they wanted to do in life. Almost anything associated with numbers and finances was at the fore of their minds every day. While others were reading any general-interest newspaper they were reading the Financial Times or another serious finance newspaper. While they were mere kids many of these professionals studied the stock market indices across Canada and in the U.S. and Europe and compared the sectors within the markets and with other world markets. They practiced strategy too.

They would select stocks from the ticker tapes and compile imaginary portfolios with a dollar amount attached to each of their investments. They would track the funds and if they had a hunch that black clouds were looming then they would sell – notionally, of course.

These same kids went on to college, worked hard at their chosen subjects and graduated to secure solid jobs with reputable accountancy firms or perhaps one of the major banking institutions.

We are talking here of the men and women across Canada who devote their lives to working with us and for us, guiding us and directing us so that our hard-earned cash is not invested in vain. They are the stewards of our savings and we should never underestimate the value of the work that they do. If you already have a financial adviser and you are very happy with that person then that is a good thing and I wouldn't encourage you to go elsewhere. But always be sure that your trust is formed on a solid base with genuine cause. In other words, never feel that your adviser is so brilliant at what they do, that they are above making an error or that they perhaps may lose their bite in the marketplace. It happens to us all at times and it can happen to them too.

They could have a domestic problem eating into their professional life and while that's tough, it's not your fault and you should never feel intimidated or reluctant to approach them or their line manager to resolve a problem. Your portfolio may be all you have and you're paying management fees to receive the best treatment that the institution can provide. If you find yourself in that situation, then speak up and ask the relevant questions. Effective, professional financial help is always available. It's out there and you should always feel free to avail yourself of it.

You should also know about the other kind of "Investment Adviser," the Johnny-come-lately type who masquerades as a professional fund manager. Fortunately, undesirable characters like these are well in the minority but they are out there. But most portfolio managers are perfectly genuine and provide a wonderful service for their clients. They are well trained, qualified and very professional in all their dealings and they would be the first to agree that there is a small percentage of financial advisers out there who cannot share the same credibility.

My strict advice to you is to read the chapter in this book on *Investment Adviser - How can I pick a good one?* and read about my experiences. Generally, I have found that the styles of advisers and fund managers differed considerably. Overall, that was a true learning phase in my life and I'm very glad to pass the information on to you because it is important that you understand what your fund manager tells you. If you don't, then tell him or her. Also, make sure that you ask all the right questions. Do not be intimidated and above all, do not be blinded with financial language that you don't understand. If you receive answers that you fully comprehend then fine but if not, then ask another question or tell your advisor that you do not understand them. Remember, it's a jungle out there and you are no monkey.

FLYING BLIND IS NOT THE WAY - chart your course
Have you only just started to think about your future years? Maybe you're in your twenties or thirties and the thought of retirement is something new to you. Maybe it was that thought that prompted you to buy this book. If so, you've made an excellent decision partly because I believe our lives have probably followed a similar pattern. I was an ordinary guy, admittedly with a good job but at that time I had never experienced real wealth or anything like that, so with meagre savings to my name I was forced into doing something about it if I was to have any hope of enjoying my future retirement days.

Many years ago, long before we had even thought about a Retirement Plan, my friend Roy and I were out playing golf. We got to the seventh hole. It was a short par three and there was a bit of a wait. Naturally, being Roy, our chat got around to finances.

He turned to me and said, "Hey, Robert. During those times when you think about your future and your eventual retirement, do you ever have a feeling of uncertainty?"

"Uncertainty?" I asked.

"Well yes," Roy continued. "Uncertainty, or perhaps worry really I suppose." "You see Robert in truth, I worry about not knowing how much I might need to live on when I retire, or how much I might actually have in my bank account for example."

"Retire?" I questioned. "Wow Roy!" I laughed. "We're barely in our thirties. Why would you be thinking about retirement?"

"Well Robert, it's going to come to us at some time. I mean, when we are old and we can't get jobs, what on earth are we going to live on?"

"Well, I haven't thought about it really." I added

Roy pressed home the point.

"For example Robert, what happens when I'm old and I run out of money? How will I manage?"

"Mm, yes. I see your point, Roy," I replied. "That could be very worrying. But to be quite honest, I have so much on my plate at the moment. What with my job and Polly and Robert junior and everything, I really don't have the time to think about retirement. I suppose I'll have to at some time, but that's light years away yet."

The point of that story is that nearly everyone is apprehensive about the future. You could call it being nervous, scared, frightened, or anything you like, but the fact remains that no one feels comfortable walking down a dark alley which is what retirement for many people is really like. You've never been there before and if you don't have a good Retirement Plan in place, just thinking about retirement is an unknown quantity. You simply don't know what to expect mainly because you haven't given the topic much thought.

No. Flying blind is not the way –.you should have a detailed plan with a clearly defined route that will provide you with the starting and finishing points, the precise direction to follow and the various waypoints so that you can progress along your charted course confidently knowing exactly where you're going and the disasters to watch out for. It is a comfort zone and I encourage you to enter it.

WILL MY PENSIONS BE O.K.? – An uncertain future prevails

No one has a crystal ball that can accurately forecast your retirement days and nobody can advise you with any degree of certainty about the future. This is because it's especially difficult to foresee any future retirement situation in today's economic climate.

Have you noticed how often pensions are now being mentioned in the newspapers and news programmes on TV? Hardly a week goes by it seems, but a news item makes some report about pensions and it is rarely good news either.

The Canadian federal government is now finding it necessary to carry out a major review of all pension plans with the possibility of increasing the age when we will be able to draw a pension. They are studying what other countries have been doing and the Canadian government is giving serious thought to increasing the retirement age, possibly to 68. If you were thinking of finishing full time employment at 65, then better think again unless you have savings sufficiently big enough to carry you for three years. Of course, it won't take effect yet but I have heard that the year 2020 was mentioned.

Increasingly, reports are saying that more and more of our pensions are being eroded or squeezed out of existence, including those in many of the larger companies. The smaller firms too are finding it necessary to re-evaluate their pension arrangements as part of their overall review of company operating costs.

Union leaders across the land have spent years negotiating improved working conditions, wages and pension benefits for millions of us but now we are told that even they are realizing that these employee benefits are under threat from employer reviews due to severe cost constraints. To put it plainly, funding an employee pension scheme has become hugely expensive and firms can no longer afford it. Unfortunately we are all living too long but this is only a part of the problem.

According to various international reports seen on corporate websites, a major shift in pension programs appears to be happening on a global basis, not just in Canada.

In April 2006 the CBC In-depth News reported that Canada was on the cusp of a "retirement revolution" and cited the baby boomers' affect on the demographics. The report stated that while 8.7 million Canadians or 38.8 percent of the working-age population will be near enough to retirement age in 2006 to give it serious thought, one third of them will conclude that they haven't set enough aside to afford to actually do it.

Do you realise what you have just read? I'll write it again and this time I'll frame it differently.

In the year 2006 nearly 40% of the working population (which is nearly NINE MILLION Canadians) will be near enough to retirement to either retire from full time employment or to give retirement some serious thought.

Furthermore, out of the aforementioned NINE MILLION Canadians, ONE THIRD of them have not yet set aside enough money to actually retire from full time employment - that's nearly THREE MILLION Canadians.

The exciting news is that YOU need NOT be one of them. But you need to start preparing your Retirement Plan – NOW!

You know there are no guarantees for anything in life, except, of course, that taxes will likely continue to rise and that we will all experience death. This is hardly news, but it should remind you that a comfortable retirement is not guaranteed for anybody.

If you're *lucky*, a happy retirement is an experience that you might get to enjoy but can you rely on luck alone? No, of course you can't.

It's probably true to say that almost everything in life is affected by luck. Timing is important too. Retirement Plans are no different. You should be extremely careful when you start planning your retirement years as there will be many pitfalls waiting for the unwary or the naïve traveller. The road to retirement is scattered with headaches and even the cleverest among us have fallen prey to some of the dangers. I will cover most of these dangers throughout the following chapters.

So, if you are now in your thirties, forties or fifties (or even younger) let me alert you to some of the steps you may need to take before it is too late.

The journey will likely cause a little pain occasionally because we live in a carefree, throw away society and we all are very much a part of it perhaps without even realizing it.

What sort of pain will there be? Well, that will vary but in short, you can choose to either have the lesser pain now or endure the greater pain later. Either way there is no avoiding it. The pain now will be when you need to keep denying yourself some of the everyday pleasures that you've gotten used to having.

You will need to discipline yourself and get used to saying "no" to treats and other purchases when all the time you really want indulge yourself and say "yes." This new routine may need to continue for many years, depending on how your life progresses. But you will enjoy watching the growth of your money tree and in the process, by denying yourself some many thousands of cups of coffee and thousands of donuts throughout your working years you may lose a few pounds and that may not be a bad thing either.

Self-constraint has a lot to do with will power and I needed plenty of that when I was working my way through my personal Retirement Plan. You will need to do the same. Believe me, it's much easier to say to yourself, "Oh, it's just a treat, I deserve it today." or "Life is so short, I may not even see my retirement." But don't! Be serious about your plan and be mature about the way you respond to it. Keep focussed on the objective – your dream retirement in the sun and a debt free lifestyle.

The choice is yours of course just as the choice was ours. You can pay now or you can pay later. Polly and I chose to pay then, hoping that the rewards later on in life would outweigh the frustration of us constantly denying ourselves some of life's little indulgences. Polly was brilliant at pulling me through the difficult times and hopefully I was able to do likewise for her. For us, it has been a team effort.

My good friend Roy found the self-discipline issue very difficult. One Saturday morning, we were all together watching our sons playing hockey at the local arena when Polly and Joan went somewhere for a chat.

"How's your retirement plan going, Robert?" asked Roy.

"Oh, Pretty good." I answered. "We watch our spending very closely so we stay within our budget each month. I think that's the name of the game. It certainly helps us anyway."

"You really have a monthly budget, Robert? On paper?"

"Of course Roy. Are you surprised that I'd go to the length of preparing a budget on a spreadsheet each month?"

"Well, do you?"

"Yes, of course I do." I laughed at the incredulous look on his face.

I explained to him how simple it was and time-efficient too. And it provided a really effective tool to properly control our monthly expenditures.

"And do you stay within those numbers?"

"Absolutely! Well, most of the time. We have to Roy. We have no choice. You see otherwise, at the end of the year we'll never have enough money for that extra mortgage payment. The plan tells us that we need to do that if we are to achieve the objective Roy." "We can't deny our money tree the food it needs to make it grow."

I explained to him for example, that if for any reason we spent over the food budget one month then the next month we'd try to under-spend. This way we hoped to keep the overall yearly costs on target. It meant saying no sometimes, in fact many times, but we knew that if we wanted that happy retirement in the sunshine then strict sacrifices would have to be made, year after year.

I realise that to you, the reader, this saving thing is now beginning to sound a bit too severe, so let me put it another way. If you prepare the Plan yourself, you build in the treats that you want and the Plan tells you what you can afford. The Plan also tells you what you *cannot* afford and so for those items, you go without.

And because you designed it all anyway, you are only agreeing to do what you wanted to do in the first place!

What I am saying is that if you are serious about having a satisfactory retirement then you need to know these things.

Creating a budget need not be a drag. For example, you can start by making it a game by guessing the costs of all of the things that you use regularly.

IMPORTANT POINT

ALWAYS LOOK AFTER THE PENNIES
AND YOU WILL FIND THAT
THE DOLLARS WILL
TAKE CARE OF THEMSELVES

After you have prepared the spreadsheet and feel happy with its contents, every time that you go on a spending spree, even just for a bottle of shampoo or a six-pack of beer, ask for a receipt and enter it in the appropriate square in your budget spreadsheet. That way you will know if you are staying within your estimates and also know if you are likely to have anything left for an extra payment against your mortgage. What is the expression? Always look after the pennies and the dollars will take care of themselves? That's it in a nutshell.

Another reason for the budget is that as you enter each purchase on the spreadsheet, you see exactly where the money goes and that's important too. I'll explain that in detail in the book and provide a grid for you as an example. You will find it quite user-friendly and you may even be in for a big surprise – you'll get a real sense of achievement each month if you finish up with an under-spent budget, knowing that it means a little bit more for your place in the sun. See. That nest egg is getting bigger already!

That is why I wanted to write this book. I wanted to try to explain in some easy-to-read way that a comfortable retirement might still be possible for you regardless of your age and in spite of what you may hear otherwise.

You may be one of those people who had almost given up on pensions, deciding instead to place your faith in your home and trust that the market value of your house or condo will provide you with a sizeable retirement nest egg. Frankly, I'm not so sure if that is a prudent course to take. Firstly, that action is violating the first principal rule of investing. You are putting all of your eggs in one basket. Your house, and as a result you are NOT diversifying.

Next, the value of real estate can go down as well as up as we have seen in the past, and if you still have a mortgage at the time you want to retire, that can create a double problem.

Another issue to consider is that quality condominiums seem to be selling for almost as much as houses and so downsizing may no longer be a feasible option when you retire unless you plan to move well out of town into a less expensive area. You may not like that idea.

No, as I said earlier, to rely on your house alone to provide you with a comfortable retirement sounds to me a bit like putting all of your nest eggs in one basket and I think it would be a wiser plan to diversify your savings.

However, as this option might still be your choice, let's take a closer look at downsizing. Suppose that you sell your house and downsize to a smaller one to generate some cash. The balance of any remaining mortgage will need to be deducted from the selling price of the house, as well as other costs such as agent fees, moving costs and lawyers' fees. Depending on the size of the mortgage, this may significantly reduce the money that you finally receive in your bank account.

Alternatively, if you opt to continue to have a mortgage when you retire, the monthly payments will cut into any pension income you expect to receive. In itself, this is a complex issue and there are many variables and unknowns, but in essence, this is definitely not my preferred option.

As I said earlier, our federal pension schemes are being reviewed by government agencies at all levels and some retirees are having their current company pensions reviewed too. Smaller, private companies are also finding it difficult to provide their staff with pension schemes, mainly due to the fact that the underlying costs of the schemes are cutting deeply into their profits.

All of this news is very worrying and quite alarming for middle-aged people and if you are one of those, how on earth can you look forward to your retirement years in your present situation? For certain, you need a personal Retirement Plan that will work for you and one that you can afford.

Think hard and carefully about *your* particular situation. Never again in your life will you be where you are now, but you know that. Time will not stand still and wait while you ponder. And, you can never go back!

Now is the time when you have a chance to do something and to make a decision that can greatly affect your future life. You've already discovered that nothing worthwhile in life comes easy. Hence the saying, "No pain, no gain."

When you get to retirement age and look back and realize just what a magnificent decision you took and the changes it made possible in your life, you will be overjoyed at the delight of financial freedom, true independence and a real sense of satisfaction when you see your savings still growing every day for the rest of your life. I feel that way now and I want you to feel it too.

I was in middle age when I was listening to that wonderful Canadian broadcaster Gordon Sinclair. He was talking about saving money and how many times he saw people wasting money on what he considered useless items. Then he came out with a sentence that changed my life. He said, "It is so much better to EARN interest than to PAY interest." I dwelt on that phrase for many days, years even. In fact, I use that same philosophy even today. I suggest you do the same.

It made such sense and the message is really so obvious. It stands to reason that if you pay out interest when you could avoid it, why would you go on doing it? It's just like throwing your money down the drain or rather, it's like you are giving your money away unnecessarily to someone else. While you get poorer - they get richer.

IMPORTANT POINT

IT IS BETTER TO **EARN**
INTEREST THAN
PAY IT!

At the time, I wondered if it could be quite that simple, so I started to learn more and more about *Interest* and discovered how banks on every street corner make it work so cleverly for them. Certainly, there aren't many of them going broke.

In particular, I was fascinated with the rapid rate of savings growth as I got to understand the immense power of *Compounding*. I found myself listening to anyone and everyone who had anything to say about saving money or paying down a mortgage, or even just paying off the loan on a credit card. I was learning a whole new vocabulary and a whole new plan. I liked it a lot because it made such good sense and it was going to make me rich in retirement.

Months later, that sentence spoken by Gordon Sinclair about *earning* interest and not *paying* interest was still in the fore of my mind. Slowly – and it was slowly, week-by-week, as I started to think about the future years and what would happen when I was old and nobody might want to employ me – my future goals started to become quite clear. I wanted to always *earn* interest and never again *pay* interest. I want your goals to become crystal clear for you too.

There is an old saying about *necessity being the mother of invention.* Well, I knew that a retirement income would be a necessity and so I decided to become inventive, in my own sort of way of course.

I also decided that if I didn't start saving soon, and if I didn't draw up a future plan, then any comfortable retirement would have to come about merely by accident and I didn't much like my chances.

I can't handle shocks too well, either, and the thought of going to the hole-in-the-wall at the local bank and finding no money left in the account to come spewing out would definitely be a shock.

And so I set about putting together a 20-year financial plan, similar to those I was already preparing every day as part of my full-time job – a plan that would ensure that Polly and I would have a retirement that could be fun and more importantly, be free from financial worries. It would need to provide us with a genuine independence and that would be welcome too. After all, I didn't want to be a burden on someone else when I got to retirement age.

That was my goal. That was *our* goal. And so with financial freedom being the cornerstone of the total edifice, the creation of my Retirement Plan virtually became my hobby for the next several months. Not a week would go by that I didn't check on our course to make sure that we were on track. I was eager to end our days of paying interest and to start earning it. I would look at our savings and our small portfolio of company shares. I would scrutinize our investments and analyze just what our financial managers were doing for us. I would study the financial columns in the newspapers, evaluate our monthly income and outgoings and determine if I could squeeze a little more out of our fun money or discretionary spending to buy some extra pension contributions. Polly and I enjoyed those days a lot. It was fun, it was easy and you can do the same.

During my working years, while regularly reviewing the master Retirement Plan I found it necessary to make one or two minor adjustments on occasion – a small shift here or a minor adjustment there to cope with a move in interest rates or a correction in the mutual fund markets – but overall, we stuck to the main philosophy of the plan. Now, in reflection, I have to say that looking around us it all seemed to work well. Very well. And Polly and I are grateful that it did.

We are now five or six years into our retirement and very much enjoying the results of our planning - and a few months ago I got to thinking,

"Why not put my plan into a book so that others might benefit from it?"

It isn't complex. You don't have to be a rocket scientist to understand it. In fact in many ways my plan is just a lot of common sense. But there are lots of things that only business experience can teach and I certainly have that experience.

By the fact that you are still with me I am led to hope that you are becoming slightly enthusiastic about all of this and that you will be eager to prepare your own personal Retirement Plan.

You've made an excellent start and now you will be anxious to know when your own retirement years can begin. Setting your retirement age can be a real thrill, believe me. I will be pleased to take you through the process in the next chapter.

Chapter two

SETTING YOUR RETIREMENT AGE
When can I afford to retire?

Typically, we Canadians all tend to think of retirement age as 65, but it doesn't have to be like that. It can be earlier or it can be later if you want it to be and don't think that later means that you have failed your objective or that life will be a drudge working at 67 or 72. You probably know someone, a retiree who is working long after they have reached 65 and this is not always because they need the money. Some people just love working, in fact with some people it becomes almost an obsession. It is their hobby if you like and they couldn't live without it especially if it is their own business and they have built it up from scratch. And as for me, I am writing a lot these days; I act in TV commercials; model in magazines and occasionally work as a secret shopper. Plus, I have a part time job working in an office of private investigators!

WHY WILL I WANT TO WORK AT 65?

In 1943, the renowned American psychologist Abraham Maslow developed a theory about human needs. He believed that as human beings one of our basic needs is to feel wanted and to be loved. This particular *need* slots in between safety or comfort and self-esteem, which are some of the other needs in his hierarchy. Anyway, perhaps the feeling of being wanted is associated in some way to the good feeling that some of us have when we are being usefully employed, even for just a few days each week.

From my vantage point, here in the early years of my retirement I can only think that life is a thrill to still be in the work force. My part time job is an area of the business world that is totally new to me and so I find my daily tasks fascinating. It is a comparatively small team that I work with, about six or seven of us providing the support for another team of about eight or so licensed private investigators who are on the road every day carrying out covert surveillance activities for our clients. Anyway, the fact remains that although I can get by comfortably on my pensions, I love my part time work and also the feeling that I get by doing something useful and making a worthwhile contribution to the company and the community in which I live.

Like me, there are many people across Canada who receive sufficient pensions to live on and also have satisfactory amounts of savings, but for a variety of reasons they choose to continue to work. You see them every day in Wal Mart, Home Depot and other large stores. Their experience is valued and they provide a good line of support for the full time staff.

They, or perhaps I should say we, look forward to spending a few days a week working with others, some of whom maybe about our own age, and I must say that frequently, for a retiree, the very act of working with younger people for a few hours a day can be very refreshing. It's amazing what you can learn about today's world.

As part of this feeling, this need to continue working, it could just be that at 65 years of age, you are simply not mentally ready to retire to a more leisurely life of playing regular golf or perhaps spending six-months of the winter away from home and the grandchildren. And that is fine. And so, now you know that some seniors really look forward to waking up every morning with a purpose… and a place to go. Perhaps, when you reach retirement age, you too may even feel that you would like to do something for a few days each week and be a part of the national group of seniors who all get a good feeling from staying in the workforce, albeit part time.

WILL AN EMPLOYER WANT ME AT 65?

Another of my good friends, almost a senior but not quite there yet is Pierre, a man from Quebec and now living in Ontario. He had worked for the telephone company for many years and when they offered him a package he decided to take early retirement. But Pierre felt that he was too young to completely retire, and in any event, his government pensions would not commence until he was sixty-five and so he wanted a part time job, or at least something to occupy his days and to help pay the bills.

Pierre quickly found a job here in Ontario where his bilingual skills were put to good use. His day starts early, which suits him just fine as he was always an early riser. His wife Monique is a teacher at junior school and as she doesn't get home until around six most evenings, Pierre has learned to cook and very much enjoys having the dinner ready on time which of course, keeps Monique very happy too.

"It's a lot different than the stressful world out there in the marketing business Robert," said Pierre in his heavy French accent. "I get home at about three in the afternoon, have a couple of hours to myself and then play chef in the kitchen." "I just love my life you know?"

"Yes, I do know." I smiled as I thought about my own part time jobs and immediately felt a contented feeling come over me. And I am happy for both Pierre and Monique. They are such nice people and they have a Retirement Plan that is working well.

We were out walking his dog last summer when Pierre turned to me and said, "You know Robert, I really love my part time job!"

"Yes, I know you do Pierre," I laughed. "You've told me many times."

He bent down and picked up a piece of dead twig from the ground. "Fetch it, Roxy" he called, as the small Miniature Snauzer dog went charging after it.

"I don't seem to feel the same pressures as I did when I was working full time."

"And you know something else, Robert. I am sure that I am less likely to have a heart attack or a stroke or something." He's probably right.

Gordon is yet another friend, who together with his wife Joan, live in the same condo building as we do. Our paths crossed as we were collecting our mail from the post room in the building. We could see through the large windows that it was snowing outside. We were happy to be in the warm comfort and were passing some time chatting about part time jobs for seniors that were advertised on the notice board. Gordon turned to me.

"When I retired Robert, I was able to be more selective in the sort of job that I wanted to do." "And as I was already receiving a pension or two, the extra income that the newly found job generated became a sort of welcome addition to the pot, so to speak."

"I'm sure," I commented.

"Every little extra I have Robert, means that I can spend a little bit more money on treats for the grandchildren." "That means a lot to Joan and me." What he said that day seemed entirely understandable.

These experiences are told here to demonstrate that while we all spend a lifetime of complaining about work and happily look forward to retirement, when we actually get there, we will likely change our minds. But it is one thing if you *want* to have a part time job and an entirely different matter if you *need* to continue to work, particularly if your retirement pension is less than you predicted for whatever the reason. But if you read this book and follow my Retirement Plan example there will be no fear of that.

Maybe your current full-time job has a supervisory function and with it the responsibility for a number of personnel. If this is the case then you will know only too well the amount of stress that comes with that position. It can also bring a variety of health problems of course, all of which send you home each day with stressful pains, headaches and other discomforts as a result of the pressure that comes with a very responsible job.

When you retire, you will discover what a relief it is to unshackle those burdens, and as a senior, you will be able to pick a part-time job that you really like, regardless of the promotion prospects. You might even be surprised as to how much some of these jobs can pay too! But whatever the amount, every little will help to supplement your pension. And it gives you the excuse to get out of the house each day and feel really important as you support those around you who depend on your friendly help in the work place.

YOUR WORK EXPERIENCE IS MORE VALUABLE THAN YOU THINK

There are many employers out there who really value the *experience* that older citizens can bring to the job. And just think. At the end of the week, in addition to the fun that you have had, you get that pay cheque!

And so, when you consider all of the various aspects of retirement, you may just feel that age does not matter. Well if it isn't age that matters then it must be something else that drives people to continue working long past their retirement age. Something has to govern the point in your life when you can retire and if it isn't age, what is it? Yes, it just has to be money.

I aimed for sixty-five as my retirement age.

"But why sixty-five?" you ask.

Well, because my work in hotels, universities and institutional management took me to different parts of the globe and as such, my pensions would necessarily originate from a variety of employers and from different countries and in various currencies.

As most of my pensions would not commence until I was aged sixty-five it seemed that the sensible thing to do was to decide that sixty-five would be the age for my retirement to commence. Of course, if retirement came earlier, then this would be a bonus I thought, but I also took the position that if retirement came later then that would be fine too. The important thing is to have sufficient funds so as to be able to do the things that you really want to do. And there might be many.

IMPORTANT POINT

RETIREMENT APPEARS TO BE THE PERFECT LIFE.

BUT WILL YOU REALLY ENJOY IT?

If you are presently working full time I know exactly what you are thinking, because when we work full time, a day off in the sun or out on the bike or off on a shopping spree sounds just great. Well of course it would because it is something different for you to do from your usual daily routine. But let's say you like shopping. I mean really like shopping. Or perhaps you were say, a professional shopper. You know, one of those people who are commissioned by well-heeled business people to make their purchases in high priced stores. Those high-flyers who have no time left out of their busy schedule for such chores as shopping. Well, if you were a professional shopper, I am told that when you take a day off, shopping is the last activity that you would wish to do.

My career was spent mostly in the hospitality business. I was operating five-star hotels and so of course, every day as a routine, I would be found dining in the restaurants and having coffee poured for me from silver jugs by immaculately dressed servers. Now this all may sound very glamorous and exciting and in some ways it can be. You never know what the day will bring and my tasks would vary from welcoming visiting heads of state to famous politicians; from commercial travellers to film stars and pretty well everybody in between. And with all of that, there is the budgeting and planning that a large hotel job demands and of course you need to take your meals throughout the day, the same as anybody else. Every meal is usually taken in the hotel because the regular guests expect to see you there and in a large hotel with many dining areas, it is a good idea to try a different place to eat each day so that you constantly view the hotel and its restaurants from a guest's perspective.

And so, when I was working full time in a large European five star hotel and I managed to get an evening off, where do you think Polly and I headed for? Right. The local "Bistro." I can't tell you how often my palette craved for beans on toast or something simple, something quite different from the rich French cuisine found in up-scale hotel restaurants. But that's how it is.

RETIREMENT - as we know it is to finish work and be free! Free to do what you like every day. Right? Well maybe. But to be honest, I thought that I would like to golf all day in the summer and to travel, seeking warmer temperatures perhaps in Florida or Spain in the winter. I dreamt of that life for most of my working days. Certainly from the age of about 45 or so and that is why I developed a 20-year plan, so all my dreams would hopefully come true. But the truth is, when I did eventually retire, I immediately applied for the first part-time job that I saw advertised in the local paper that caught my eye! I don't know why I did it, I just did. Was I mad? Again, I don't know.

Within a week I was back in the workforce. But this time it was different. It was like being on a vacation, and I got paid for doing it.

Question: "Why did I rejoin the workforce so soon?" Answer: "I haven't a clue!" But here I am, more than four years later, still doing it and loving it, probably due to the fact that there are no serious responsibilities and so, in addition, I have enough free time that I can have a few other part time jobs that I enjoy. They vary tremendously, from my morning job in the private investigators' office to acting in TV commercials. And now I find myself writing! I also do Mystery Shopping.

Almost none of these jobs have anything to do with my career appointments but even so, I take each of them seriously. I find them fun and I love doing every one of them, in fact, they are almost like a hobby to me. So much for my dream of retirement and being full of free time! But I do still play regular golf. I also take my son fishing occasionally, or rather perhaps these days he takes me fishing. Robert junior is 47.

HOW RETIREMENT HAS CHANGED

You know, years ago, retirement was all about an old man trying to keep busy with his newly found free time. This new, strange vacuum in his life was filled in a variety of ways and frequently his days were spent by working in the garden or the basement or perhaps by taking up an indoor or outdoor hobby. Or maybe even taking his wife out for lunch and a shopping trip. Well, that was fine for that time and for those people. Generally speaking, it had been the man-of-the-house who had gone out to a place of work and meanwhile, the woman was expected to work at home. And many years later, when the man reached 65 or 70, it was also quite expected that the man got to retire from work while the woman of the house was left to continue working! Who said, "A woman's work is never done?" Yes, a woman was expected to carry on working in the home even though the kids had flown the nest. Unfortunately our great-grandmothers and their mothers before them rarely saw retirement, as we know it today.

But now that we are in the twenty-first century things are quite different. We look different, we act different and we even feel different.

How lucky we are. If funds allow, adults everywhere can look forward to enjoying a future retirement, comfortable for each of them. "Equal *rest* for work of equal value!"

When you think about it, the types of jobs that women did in the home in those days very often provided them with a skill that often went unnoticed. To actually run a home necessarily indicates that in some way you would need to have some management ability. And if you were provided with an amount of money with which to buy food, household goods and clothes, then you would need some budgeting knowledge so as to ensure that you spent less than what was in your pocket.

When we read about how things were many years ago and the history of our recent ancestors, it becomes quite clear that many women practiced every day a ritual that we know today as multi-tasking. Many women were administrators in their own right, running the many affairs of the home so as to ensure that everyone had what they needed. It was important that meals were on the table on time. Remember also that families tended to be much larger in those days. Is it little wonder therefore that now, almost everywhere, women make a great contribution to the world of business and commerce and indeed, regularly find themselves involved in Board-Room appointments?

CAN I DEPEND ON MY COMPANY OR FEDERAL PENSION?

Today, in the twenty-first century, the business world has become highly competitive and in the global village accountants make many of the major decisions. Yes! The bottom-line profit levels are increasingly influencing the decision-makers. So it was only a question of time before, along with reviews of other costly expenditures, the true costs of employee pensions would also be scrutinised by company accountants.

Slowly, you are all being squeezed out of company pension plans and even recently, Statistics Canada reported that government pension plans too are under review. We see only too often that companies are cutting their costs in their departments and at all levels. The future for federal pensions is being seriously threatened.

All of you who are still working full time and under retirement age are at risk and you need to seriously review what you are doing for yourselves to provide a secure future for yourselves in your retirement. You must now take it upon yourselves to make provision for your retirement years. No longer can you rely on help from others it seems. You must act NOW!

The newspapers remind us frequently that pensions are being eroded in a number of different ways including the ever-rising cost of living. Just think. If the money in your savings account is earning three percent each year but the cost of living is rising three and a half percent each year, where exactly are you? How much will you have left in real buying terms after just ten years? Where will *you* be? After your savings totals have been re-calculated in future years, do you really think that you will be ahead?

If you do not think that you will be ahead with the passing of time then shouldn't you be considering investing in something else? Something that will provide a return each year that is at least equal or higher than the annual increases announced in the cost of living index?

Look! I cannot overstress the urgency of the matter here. I cannot say it any clearer. The earlier you get started the sooner you can take advantage of the power of compounding and so see you earning interest on interest.

If you are ready then let me take you to the moment of planning. Let us discuss the age at which you will feel comfortable retiring, the time in your life when your financial position will permit you to be free from being a slave to a pay-cheque.

As I stated earlier, I don't profess to have a secret formula, but what you can be sure of is to read about the plan that I created for myself – a successful, self-created plan that got Polly and me to a happy retirement in 20 years or so and really, isn't that what you want for yourself?

I am an ordinary person, probably a bit like you. And now that we are retired from full time employment, my wife Polly and I enjoy a similar lifestyle as we did when we were working although of course our monthly income is significantly reduced. But our monthly living costs are well below our income and we have no money worries. We have almost everything that we want and we have no complaints. Now, doesn't that sound the sort of retirement that would suit you?

At this point, I should say that throughout some of our married life Polly did not work. In fact, she worked for about 12 years altogether, and at one point for a six-month period we actually depended on her income to make our mortgage payments. We had one child who was very undemanding and while he was not a strain on our finances, nevertheless, the additional costs were still there.

The *Edmond Financial Group* reported in 2006,

"Based on 2004 budget guides the cost of raising a boy child to age eighteen is $166,971.00." I suspect that the cost to raise a girl child is similar.

I was never a lawyer or accountant or for that matter anything that brought in a fantastic income. No! I was in hotel management and the wages were anything but above average. But the benefits were sometimes good. We travelled a great deal and sometimes we "lived in" which saved us many mortgage payments. Of course, the downside of this is that if you find yourself out of a job, you will also find yourself standing with your suitcases at the end of the street with nowhere to go. And in addition, we missed many years of any capital appreciation that comes from owning a property such as a house or a condo.

IMPORTANT POINT

STRATEGIC PLANNING

IF YOU DON'T KNOW WHERE YOU'RE GOING

THEN ANY ROAD WILL TAKE YOU THERE

My major strength in my hotel and institutional management career was future financial planning. Managing a hotel isn't just about providing rooms, food and beverages although I agree that at times it might look that way.

You need to be sure that when your guests arrive the rooms will be ready. Further, that the restaurants and bars will be properly prepared and staffed by employees, all of whom have been thoroughly trained. Moreover, that all of the staff are fairly managed by supervisors who conduct their departments in a professional manner.

If some or none of this is correctly planned and managed then disaster will surely strike at some point. It might be a fire. It might be food poisoning, or it might be a freak accident such as someone tripping over something in a guest room. To assist hotel managers in their planning there is an old phrase and the sooner it is learnt and adhered to the better the chances of operating an hotel effectively.

I remember it as if it were yesterday (with apologies to Robert Louis Stevenson, 1850-1894) as I sat in the large windowless classroom. It was in the early eighties and I was attending a management-training course. In particular, we were discussing Strategic Planning and how to prepare an effective long-term financial plan when the facilitator turned and pointed at me.

"Robert." He said.

I stiffened. I felt that I was about to be embarrassed in front of my own work colleagues.

"Robert. When you develop a long-term plan, do you think it is important to focus on your objective, and if so, then why?" she asked.

I thought for a moment.

"So that you have a clear vision of the goal?" I answered.

She turned away and walked to the front of the class. When she arrived at the point where she could continue to walk no further she turned. She looked at all of the students in the class, turning her head as she did so. We all waited for her comment.

"If you don't know where you are going then any road will take you there," she stated. "In other words, rather than take a straight line to your goal you may become distracted and finish up taking a wavy line instead. This will waste time and possibly resources. And time is money." She emphasised the point.

She concluded, "And we all know that the shortest route between two points is a straight line, don't we?"

And so, this simple statement learnt many years ago has always been remembered by me and passed on to others. It possibly originated in one of those management books that we all read during those days. *A Passion for Excellence* and *In Search of Excellence* were best selling books at that time written by Tom Peters and published by Random House Inc. Managers in all types of occupations were buying them and rarely was a management-training programme given without reference to Tom Peters. Those books were full of many inspiring ideas that if followed, could likely provide the reader with an edge as to how to generate increased business as a result of going the extra mile. But more than that, they helped to teach the reader to plan effectively for the future and to manage their day-to-day responsibilities in a truly professional manner. That was my job. Planning and management, and so I needed all the help I could get.

Anthony Robbins was also skilled in helping to unlock the door to success for many people and indeed, still does. He is able to thrill audiences by showing them just how much anyone's life can change, by making a small adjustment now, and now is the operative word. And in some ways, that is what I am attempting to do too. To You! I am trying to get you to consider your future now and to take some important decisions before it is too late, because I know, that for every month that you delay making contributions to a pension plan, you are losing out on many thousands of dollars that you will not have when you are my age. And you can never recapture the time that is lost. It is gone forever.

I want to introduce into your mind how important it is to make a relatively small adjustment now so that your years ahead can provide you with the pleasures you seek. Believe me, it is never too soon to start saving. But you must start NOW!

And so, in those days, I developed good and effective planning skills, some might even say outstanding, not only for financial planning but for other important aspects of hotel keeping too. My schemes included a complete range of staff training programmes, and so, in addition to being good at their jobs, my staff were trained to be better prepared for the future needs of the hotel guests. They too learned to plan well and be prepared to deal with a hotel fire or perhaps a heart attack victim. They learnt first aid and basic fire fighting skills from the fire marshal's office. Local medics and fire fighters were always very pleased to be a part of the training scheme. I established a Health & Safety Committee and our monthly meetings always included regular visits from outside professionals to provide the staff with good professional training and practical demonstrations.

Other planning skills included "how to save a wedding cake."

When the weight of the top two tiers forces the supporting pillars to penetrate into the main cake at the base, there is an emergency procedure that can be implemented so that the crisis can be minimized and the wedding day saved. (This highly skilled procedure can bring a special level of comfort to the Bride's Mother!)

Future planning for all emergencies can help save the day and in some instances, may avoid major family embarrassments or even save a life.

And so, for the operation of a successful hotel or institution it is vital that a good financial plan is in place. This will ensure that the purchasing levels are controlled and that guest rates for accommodation, food and beverages can remain competitive. This in turn, will ensure a high occupancy percentage that will surely satisfy the shareholders who are the owners of the hotel. Yes, a good financial plan must include effective cost and inventory controls so as to ensure that profits are maximized and the shareholders are able to re-invest. This will help to maintain high visual standards as well as providing a team of well-paid, quality professional staff.

But enough about hotels. Hopefully, the examples will help you to see that if you do not plan for the future then you will likely arrive somewhere by accident. "Any road will get you there," and where you finish up may NOT be the place where you want to be.

My career as a manager of hotels, hospitals and college institutions forced me to develop an expertise in long term financial planning and cost-effective budgeting for large operational departments across the globe. Budgeting, simply put, is estimating the cost of an item and controlling the underpinning financing of it. You all do this every day.

For example, let's say that your train fare to work and back is $10.00 and that the cost of a newspaper is $1.00. Add to this the cost of a counter lunch, say $10.00, and say two coffees at $2.00 each. The total daily cost for you will be $25.00. You also know that you will need to pay in cash or charge the amount, which will be $25.00 each working day.

If you work a five-day week, you must budget to spend a weekly amount of $125.00 for these items and assuming that you work for 48 weeks each year, the annual budget will be $6,000.00.

To pay for that cost you will need to earn around $8,000.00 before income tax. This is just to cover your expenses for you to go to your job each day! Well, hopefully, you all earn more than $8,000.00 each year otherwise there would be little point in going to work!

PLANNING TO SUIT YOUR LIFESTYLE

Personal planning for your future retirement is very similar. It just means that you need to budget for your long-term needs rather than just a year.

Future planning will almost surely include some income that you don't know about and can only estimate. Also, there will be unknown costs that you will be unable to forecast accurately. Everyone has different needs, but the things that you enjoy throughout your working life are also the things that most of you hope to continue to enjoy when you are retired.

We hear a lot these days about LIFESTYLE! Certainly, the lifestyle that we get used to we usually like, although the lifestyle that we experience when we are maturing through adulthood with growing children may not be the sort of lifestyle we will want to continue when we retire.

Empty Nesters will perhaps want to dispose of their house and settle into a more compact, smaller home such as a condo or a town house. This may provide them with all of the amenities that they will need in their new life. It may even provide a cash surplus from the sale of the house. To be achieved, this lifestyle should be planned for and usually planned for well in advance.

Almost certainly, the over-riding factor that will govern the kind of life that Empty Nesters will have will be the finances. There is no question, that if the money is there, then all that both he and she dreams of in retirement can be realized. Unless you inherit a legacy or an unexpected windfall, this is usually only achievable from good planning. But you need to start NOW!

When you eventually get to retirement it will be very unusual if your monthly income will be as much as it was during the final years of your working life. While this can be worrying, the good news is that as a result of this you will likely be in a lower income tax bracket. This is an interesting point when you think about it and worth reviewing in more detail for a moment.

If, as a result of having a lower monthly income when you retire you will pay less income tax, isn't this an important goal that you should consider? The answer is "yes." But, I hear you ask, if I plan to have a lower income for the sake of paying less income tax, how will I pay for all the costs that will be incurred to provide me with my preferred lifestyle? The mortgage, the car payment, the monthly costs for heating, water and light, the telephone bill, loans on credit cards and the costs for vacations, they all add up and they all need to be paid for. So how will you get around this or as they say, "Square the circle?"

IMPORTANT POINT

PLAN TO HAVE NO MORTGAGE

WHEN YOU REACH 65

When I was faced with this problem several thoughts came to my mind mainly triggered by the glaring fact that the amount of income

I would need should at all costs, be kept to a minimum. Which brings us very conveniently to another important point. Plan to have no mortgage when you retire.

This will be a major key in your Retirement Plan. If you can get your head around the idea that you will own your house free and clear of any mortgage at the age when you expect to retire, then you are a long way down the road to accomplishing the number-one main objective in my plan. You need to be debt-free when you get to 65, or earlier if you plan to retire earlier.

So. If you want to retire at 50 - and why not, then read on. The contents of my book could determine whether or not that might be possible for you. You may be pleasantly surprised, or you may be in for a shock!

Chapter Three
A WOMAN'S PERSPECTIVE

THE TEAM STAR

During my working years in business I was sometimes reminded by that well versed saying, "Behind every successful man is a woman." I suppose in some ways, it can be said that my life has had its occasional successes and without wishing to sound patronising, it is true to say that Polly has had much to do with it. She has always been there for me during every one of our forty some years together, and it has been from her that I have learnt much about life in general and women's special issues in particular.

Polly is an independent thinking person who, when I met her, had direct charge of over thirty staff. I think that her management style was one of the attractions that caught my eye. She seemed so comfortable with herself, planning and supervising her way through her working day and being a student of psychology, perhaps it occurred to my subconscious mind that I would like her to plan and supervise our future life together. Anyway, we married and shared what life threw at us (and some of it was not too pleasant), and together as a dream team, we have raised our glasses to celebrate many a New Year, a birthday or some other happy occasion.

For over forty years we have worked hard and been united as a family which was especially important if our Retirement Plan was to work. When there are two of you, it is essential that you both feel the same way about saving for your retirement. As a woman, Polly's strong role in our successful project reminded me that all women have special qualities of one kind or another and so it was natural that I should want to write a chapter to discuss the issues especially important to women. To openly discuss some of them too so as to help those of you who want to prepare your own personal Retirement Plan and save for your future years. Perhaps I should hurriedly add that men too should read this chapter as many of the principles discussed apply to everyone.

WOMAN'S STRUGGLE THROUGH THE YEARS

I recently heard on the radio an Islamic man talking about his great concern for the image that many non-Muslim people have regarding the manner in which Islamic men treat their women. "Islamic men could only ever treat women with gentle kindness," he said, "for it is a woman who gives every man his birth and infant nurture." He underlined, "It is a woman who gives every Muslim man his life and will bear his children."

That statement seems to be a doctrine that most men could readily subscribe to.

In these early years of the twenty-first century, society sees many more women securing senior positions in business, industry and politics, especially in the western parts of the world.

This is happening, not because a woman owns the company although in truth many do, but it is occurring due to more and more women enjoying the new found freedom and the opportunities to receive a higher education that they now have as part of the equal opportunity to pursue their goal and reach their potential.

Women are at last liberated. They compete head-to-head with their male counterparts for the top jobs and are winning many of the competitions fairly in their own right.

Statistics Canada wrote in March 2006: *Women have increased their representation in several professional fields in recent years. Indeed, women currently make up over half those employed in both diagnostic and treatment positions in medicine, related health professions and in business and financial professional positions. There has also been a long-term increase in the share of women employed in managerial positions. In 2004, 37% of all those employed in managerial positions were women, up from 30% in 1987. However, all this growth occurred in the early part of this period. The share of management positions accounted for by women actually dipped slightly between 1996 and 2004. As well, among managers, women tend to be better represented in lower-level positions as opposed to those at more senior levels. Women also remain very much a minority among professionals employed in the natural sciences, engineering and mathematics.*

The Daily Report – Women in Canada - Stats Canada –
March 7, 2006

The members of the suffragette movement were some of the early activists to raise their voices in favour of women's rights. Since those early days each generation has increasingly produced women who have stood tall to claim an equal stake in managing almost every career field from industry to government, from retail mega-stores to the military and pretty well everything in between.

Many women throughout the world are now receiving equal recognition for the major contribution that they make alongside their male counterparts. They share good working conditions and fair treatment in the workplace and this has progressed as part of the continual struggle for social justice everywhere.

During these changing times we see the baby boomers emerging too. They herald the coming of those people born between 1946 and 1964. The anticipated great surge in the population numbers has for years, been closely studied everywhere by sociologists, endeavouring to predict the effect that they would have on the economy. Producers of goods and services worldwide would need to gear up so as to be ready for the population bulge and be able to tailor their production lines in styles and volumes commensurate with the unprecedented demand.

While I expect that both genders will find interest in this chapter, I wrote it especially for women because as you will see, there are special considerations exclusively for women in matters relating to retirement planning.

OLDER WOMEN FACE POVERTY ALONE –It's Official

According to news reports we are told that it is not unusual to hear of cases where Canadian women are living in poverty in their old age and frequently for reasons that are beyond their own control. It may be due to poor planning in earlier years, when as a married woman, she and her husband made poor decisions regarding their finances. But all sorts of pressures are placed on couples with families persuading them that they should "enjoy life now and save for retirement later."

It should be noted here that for every five-years you put off starting to save (for your retirement), you actually double the amount of cash you will need to invest so as to obtain the same result. That's partly due to the power of compounding, which means that money grows progressively faster and faster over time. Thus, the shorter the time you have, the smaller the opportunity to rapidly increase your savings.

So again you are reminded. It is never too soon to start saving. You must start NOW!

The statistics tell us that women live longer than men and that many women find themselves in a lonely and destitute situation after having spent a comfortable, happy lifetime bringing up a family. Part of this dilemma is created by the unfair practice that continues in our society where many women receive a lower wage than a man for doing the same job with identical responsibilities. Or perhaps where a pension for a woman was not available.

Also, when a marriage breaks down, we are told that in many cases the woman finds herself with the responsibility of raising the children from the marriage without the benefit of receiving any support from a disappearing husband.

There have been numerous cases where two healthy adults will agree that one of them will stay home and care for the children while the other continues with their career. However, in the event of a breakdown in the relationship, if it was a woman who was the children's caregiver, she would be the one who finds that she must now re-enter the workforce. In such a case, her retirement plan would need very special action and fast.

These various situations and others all had a compelling impact on my writing this chapter and I attempt to discuss most of the issues that could arise when a woman considers the preparation of a Personal Retirement Plan.

Here is another extract from a Statistics Canada report that is particularly significant. You may find it riveting while many readers may find it troubling. For ease of understanding the meaning of the statistics, you can substitute the word *median* for the word *average* if you like – the result will be roughly the same.

It says, *Median family income declined continuously among senior women who became widowed, especially compared with women who remained married. (The median is the amount where one-half of the population is above, and the other half is below.) The impact of widowhood was immediate.*

In the year before their husbands died, senior women had a median income of $24,400. One year after they were widowed, this amount had declined 1.6% to $24,000. Among other senior married women, median family income remained unchanged at $26,800. Based on these median values, it might be assumed that widowhood brings only a small change in living standards.

However, five years down the road, median family income had fallen for both widows and senior women who remained married. Among widows, median family income declined 9.8%, more than six times greater than the 1.5% decline among senior women who were not widowed.

The study also found that not only did the standard of living for these widows decline, but more of them also fell below the low-income threshold as a result of widowhood. And once these senior widows were in low income, it was very difficult for them to climb out.

Stats Canada – The Daily – July 22, 2004. The economic consequences of widowhood, 1990-2001

To me, this report seems very typical of what we are being told on a regular basis these days and has very serious implications. This is just the sort of stuff that worries me deeply because too many people are not taking the threat of disappearing pensions personally. They are assuming that they will be fine and that the report is referring to someone else.

I think that it is important to dissect this report a little. I really want you to be clear about what is being said here.

It states that five years down the road, (presumable 5-years after a woman has been widowed) *"the median family income declined 9.8%, more than six times greater than the 1.5% decline among senior women who were not widowed."*

But interestingly, this is what the report does *not* say. If, for example the average annual cost of living index is 3% during the said 5-year period, the living costs will have increased 15%. Meanwhile, it states that the widows' income will have declined nearly 10%.

For clarity, let us view it in a different form.

Immediately after widowhood:

Monthly Income:	$2,033, ($24,400/year)
Monthly Living Costs:	$2,000 ($24,000/year)
RESULT: Monthly *Surplus:*	$33 ($396/year)

Five years later:

Monthly Income:	$1,834 ($22,008/year)
Monthly Living Costs:	$2,300 ($27,600/year)
RESULT: Monthly *Deficit*:	$466 ($5,592/year)

Serious stuff indeed, and while the report does not state in detail why the widows' income declines, I think that we can safely assume the reason is that 50% of the family has been removed from the equation and taken most of their pension with them. But the point here is that any *increase* in the cost of living can and probably will - greatly and quickly erode any other savings that the widow may have put aside. Is it any wonder that many elderly Canadian women find themselves living in poverty after having lived a fairly prosperous life when compared with women living in the other parts of the world?

After reading the above report from Statistics Canada you may feel it prudent to immediately review your own retirement savings arrangements. For example, if you already have a plan then I would certainly urge you to consider making an increase to your monthly contributions if you are able. You may be very sure that one day, and it will arrive quite soon, you will be retired and it may be with a spouse or partner or it may be alone. And while your retirement years may start out with somebody else, it could happen that a large part of your retirement could be spent alone.

Whatever your future situation, you can be sure that you will never have *too much* money. But you may have too little. This is why I encourage you to work hard so as to prepare a fat retirement nest egg and a retirement plan that will work for you and give you that happy dream in prosperity. The alternative may be a miserable nightmare in poverty. But truly, you must start NOW!

ALONE AND ZEALOUS – The A-Z of the single woman is discussed

The successful creation and achievement of a retirement plan for a *single* woman is a particularly special case because perhaps more than anybody, the single woman maybe more vulnerable to financial distractions so as to fill the void in her life. Certainly widows are at extreme risk as we have just learned.

The single woman needs to create and maintain a clear focus on her personal savings and investments so that she can be assured of that happy retirement at the end of her working life. She cannot afford to take someone else's word as the gospel truth for there are many stories alluding to trusting single women who find that their reliability has been taken advantage of.

Perhaps not everyone will appreciate this important point and so I want to take a little time here to delve into the issues and see what we find.

If you are a single woman you will know very well that there are many problems that you need to regularly face without the advantage of having the support and guidance of a second person with whom you live. When you have a problem that needs solving your discussion group consists of you and you alone. How often you wish that there were somebody else that you could trust and with whom you could share confidences or troubles. But perhaps you once had a relationship that didn't work and you experienced pain and anguish but now you have emerged as a stronger human being. We had a friend in this situation and she said that she found a renewed peace with herself and was able to live her life as a more confident woman stronger in the knowledge that she had survived where others might have failed.

You may have tested relationships along the way but thus far you have found them to be empty and unfulfilling and so, at this particular time in your life you have decided that they are not for you.

Perhaps you have a child or children that accompany you through life's journey and you find that you benefit so much from their innocence, their love and their total dependency. The fact that their young minds know that you will be there for them every day fills you with pride and joy and above all else, the bond you have needs to remain sacrosanct. What supreme happiness they give you between the times when they provide you with worry, anger and fret. You love them to bits and demonstrate that to them regularly in so many ways. In return, they reward you with the loving and cosy company that you need and long for.

As they play, you gaze at them and let your mind run years ahead, imagining them as perhaps a famous entertainer or a successful businessperson or even a world famous politician. And then, when you come back down to earth you realise that you just want them to be happy and healthy, perhaps to be married one day and have a house full of kids. Or just to be loved by someone of their own kind. You envy them their youth and even perhaps their opportunities to be connected with another and have the companionship that you yearn for so much.

Here is another reason why it is important for you to have a personally devised retirement financial plan. Not so that when you are older, you can buy your friends but so that you will be able to buy your lifestyle and have the necessary funds to provide yourself with the protection that you may need in later years. The future will slip by very quickly and you need to be sure that you can be financially independent throughout your working life as well as into your retirement years.

EVERY WOMAN NEEDS HER OWN PENSION PLAN

If you are presently in the happy position of being financially independent, you will be able to pick and choose your friends based on the grounds that you like them and have something in common with them, not because you need a person who can provide you with a meal ticket or who can throw a crumb to you sometimes. Saving money in your own account can really happen for you, and you can be just as strong as a woman who is part of a couple. In fact, there are many advantages for you in your present situation that a woman in a relationship may not have.

For example, as a single person living alone, you are in control. You are the one and only person who makes any decisions regarding your life, your future, where you live, with whom you live, how you live and what job you do. You can decide when you go out and where you will go. You don't have to ask anybody or to receive anyone's consent. You just make your decision and off you go.

Many of your friends may not tell you this but in truth they may envy you enormously. They feel obligated to put up a front and tell the world that their relationship is fine when perhaps in reality, if they could extricate themselves, they would pack up and go tomorrow.

Financially, you have some advantages too. You don't ever need to squabble with anyone because of what was spent out of last week's budget on that little black number or a jacket that you didn't really need. You never need to sneak into the bedroom and stealthily creep to your favourite secret place to hide away those new boots and that new pair of pants that you just couldn't resist. And when it comes to deciding on a trip somewhere, you can make that choice yourself and go with whomever you like, never needing to consult someone before agreeing to participate in the venture. And you can decide to cancel it too if you wish to, without thinking of anyone else.

IMPORTANT POINT

AN OPPORTUNITY MISSED

IS AN OPPORTUNITY LOST

FOR EVER!

MAKE WINDFALL OPPORTUNITIES COUNT BIG

So supposing for a moment that you had arranged with a friend to go off on a skiing trip to Whistler, B.C., or on a week's break to Florida or whatever, and you had saved about $3,500 cash to pay for the experience. You get a call one evening to say that the friend is very sorry but they need to cancel their vacation and the trip is off. You were due to visit the travel agent next week to pay for the trip and so you still have the money. What will you do with the $3,500? Let's consider some of your options and there are lots of them.

i. Spend it on a trip to go elsewhere.

ii. Trade in your car and add the $3,500 to the down payment for that new red sporty number you saw at the auto dealers last week.

iii. Bank the $3,500 and spend it in dribs and drabs as your heart desires.

iv. Use the $3,500 as an extra payment against your mortgage.

v. Invest the $3,500 in a tax sheltered RRSP for say, thirty-five years with a reputable and trusting fund manager.

Most people in your position would select either options i, ii, or iii, but as I am here to persuade you to make wise financial decisions for the *long* term, I have to tell you that they are definitely not for you.

(O.K. so I am boring. But I am having a great retirement with lots of money!)

If you have an open mortgage on your property, Option iv could definitely save you many thousands of dollars over a period of say thirty years depending on the small print written in your Mortgage Agreement. Yes, it could certainly be a good idea to discuss this option with your mortgagor.

If you are thirty-five and thinking that Option v would serve you well in the long term then I believe that you are probably on the right track. The sum of $3,500 if invested with an aggressive fund manager for 35 years in a tax sheltered RRSP with an average return of about 9.5% could reward you with about $84,000.00 when you are seventy-years old. Now that would make a nice birthday present wouldn't it?

Take a look at the FINANCIAL CHART headed *Investment Example – Save $3,500 and Invest it for 35 Years* for a closer look at this opportunity.

If you feel really zealous and are able to repeat that exercise for the same period of time investing $3,500 for *each* of those thirty-five years, when you reach 70, with favourable conditions you could have around $926,000. You are almost a millionaire with a retirement to die for!

Take a look at the FINANCIAL CHART headed *Investment Example – Save and Invest $3,500 Each Year for 35 Years* in this chapter for a closer look at this opportunity.

PERSONAL SECURITY – Protection for # 1, that's YOU

This book is about you - preparing for your future years and the necessary steps that you should be taking now so as to build sufficient funds for the lifestyle that you want later. In this chapter, we have been discussing the role of the woman and I have purposely drawn out the differences between a woman who lives alone and a woman who lives with another person because the woman in each situation will necessarily have different needs, especially when it comes to preparing a Retirement Plan.

The differences expressed in the needs of the two groups may be simply that and in fact, when it comes to comparing other things such as characteristics, personality and traits there may be no variances whatsoever.

The woman who lives alone may well be gregarious and might have many friends with whom to share an active social life but when the sun starts to set and the day draws to a close she must return to her home, alone. Thank goodness for the kids and pets who can snuggle up for a cuddle or two, and don't cry for her. Better this life than being in a violent relationship that you fear to the extent that going home means forcing yourself to reluctantly travel in a direction that you dread. This situation can present a feeling of unknown suspicion when you arrive at your destination and slide the key in the latch. If you have been down this road then you know what I am talking about only too well.

The woman who resides with another may in fact live exactly this sort of a life, and yes, tragically many women genuinely fear for their existence. They wake-up each day with a violent person as their bedfellow, frightened by the regular ultimate threats that they receive and to such an extent, that they stay in their situation and blame themselves for causing the constant barrage of physical onslaught. They are brainwashed daily to believe this, we are told. Too scared are they to leave this frightening mess with their kids and start anew.

In a recent United Nations paper the Secretary General noted that in the United States a woman is beaten by her partner every 18 minutes, and while those statistics may be quite different in Canada,

closed doors guard many secrets. Yes, the woman who lives alone
is often envied by many of her sisters.

A woman who lives with a partner however and who enjoys a
happy relationship may also have many advantages. I know that our
good friends Del and Dave have been together for years and even
though they confess to fighting like cat and dog from time to time, they
enjoy the making up, warmly embracing and gazing lovingly into each
other's eyes. (So they tell us!)

"Just wait until I get you home." Del says threateningly. Well!
Who knows what that statement really means and what really goes on
when they get home and close the outside doors behind them.

Some couples stay together for life, providing a situation where
someone is always close-by to care for each one of them in times of
sickness or sorrow. There is always someone to share their secrets and
someone to share their joy.

In a long-term relationship there is the probability that the two
grow increasingly alike as the years pass and in their later years they
may think the same and even be able to guess what the other is
thinking. I know that this happens with Polly and me sometimes.

IMPORTANT POINT

THERE IS A DIFFERENCE BETWEEN
INVESTING AND GAMBLING

1	Risk level	10
Investing		Gambling

But whatever situation you personally are in at this point in
your life, it may not be forever. It is amazing how quickly things can
change and you don't need me to tell you that people can change too.
We all change and sometimes it is not for the better either and if
disaster strikes and a separation takes place for whatever reason, even

through a tragic death or perhaps our partner walking out of the relationship, the fact is there and there is nothing you can do to change your newly found situation. What I am trying to say is that while you may have a partner today, you should certainly plan ahead and think about what you might want to do if you were suddenly left alone. Maybe your partner has already done this without informing you.

SECRETS? SO WHAT!

Do you trust your partner? Really trust them? How would you feel if you found that they had been secretly hoarding money away for ten years in a separate bank account or a secret grubby paper bag in an unused closet in the basement? It happens more frequently than you may think and you might even know of someone who does just this.

We know someone who did this, mainly because her marriage was going nowhere and a split in the future seemed inevitable. Her husband was very wealthy and had everything in his name. Fearing for her uncertain future and the risk that she may be left with nothing from the marriage, our friend secretly opened a bank account and made regular deposits to build herself a nest egg. She actually carried out this plan on the advice of a professional friend.

Being the nice person she was however, her conscience would not permit her to continue with the deceit and so, after about a year, she began the task of dismantling her savings and returned every nickel into the housekeeping funds. Some people would say that she was crazy to replace the money but it was her choice and at least she could sleep at night with a clearer conscience. But what would you do if you thought your partner was stashing money away?

You may not like the idea of confrontation but what would you do? Could you openly confront them face-to-face and virtually accuse them of stealing from your mutually shared savings funds? Or perhaps you have already. Or maybe you yourself have opened a private bank account - hiding money for a rainy day. If the circumstances were right would it be such a stupid idea? Particularly if you were already buying the odd piece of clothing or a pair of shoes and when the opportunity presented itself, quietly stashed them in the closet without saying anything. So. Why not cash? What is the difference? You see, fundamentally you agree with me that the important thing for you to do is to protect yourself and to secure your own future. And in my opinion, providing what you do is legal I have no problem with that.

You wouldn't be the first woman to find herself with a handful of unpaid bills, a house to maintain, kids to raise and a disappearing spouse who vanished into thin air with someone half his age. If putting away a few dollars every month or so helps to provide you with the financial (and mental) security that you want and a happy future for you and your kids then I say, "fine!" Charity starts at home and if you have the smarts – who is to say that your partner or spouse isn't doing the same thing?

If you are working and contributing to the joint household income, even by doing the household chores, bringing up the kids and preparing the meals then by all the reports that I read, it is considered neither stealing nor criminal. There would seem nothing wrong with it and if after twenty or thirty years you find that things have turned out just fine then what a pleasant surprise it will be for your spouse or partner. You can treat them to an anniversary present or a birthday surprise party or a cruise; and with the rest, well you may want to think about that one. Maybe you will consider disclosing only part of the booty. That would leave a little nest egg for you to turn to if you were left alone and you were eighty. Not for you an impoverished widowhood!

HOW CAN I ACHIEVE SUCCESS? – Many do, why not you?
When I think of successful women I am reminded by another old saying.

"If you look good you feel good - and if you feel good you do good."

I don't know where it originated and now it may sound a bit outdated but somewhere through the haze of time I think that there is a bit of truth there that holds up. It especially seems appropriate for special occasions such as going for a job interview or sitting for a special examination or a test. Anything that helps provide you with that little bit of extra confidence may be just the extra zest you need to assure you of that success you yearn for.

Many women have experienced success regularly throughout the ages although perhaps not made to fully appreciate their accomplishments by those around them - no diplomas or bits of paper to say that they had excelled when nevertheless they had. Unfortunately nobody bothered to tell them and so, over the years many women were never told of their successes. They were left to guess if they had achieved the great things they wished for.

Their thoughts (and hopes) were perhaps only confirmed when they saw how their children had grown from gawky, spider-like kids into beautiful young human beings bearing the likeness of their parents or siblings, playing piano, singing in a choir or excelling on the sports field.

Yes women have always been achievers but now in a new age, while their success is still recognized on the domestic front, fresh opportunities in the world of business have been presented to them. Women almost everywhere have risen to the challenge by competing for jobs in what was always a man's world. Politicians, leaders in industry, engineers, architects and airline pilots are but a few of the top jobs that women have taken on and excelled in.

Take the fairytale story of the apprentice ladies hairdresser, aged seventeen who was fascinated with flight. Such was her passion that she studied to be an air traffic controller and graduated through her classes to become a very good one. Not satisfied with that, she then went to flight school and learned to fly. Small private planes at first and after a few years she moved up to big commercial passenger jets and landed a job as a co-pilot with a major airline. "Truly amazing" thought her family. And told her so.

Our hairdresser heroine was so encouraged with her progress and the accompanying praise, that within a short period of time she qualified as a full pilot and when the airline merged with British Airways, Barbara Harmer was selected out of a group of 3,000 pilots to train and become Concorde's first and only woman pilot!

There are and have been many outstanding Canadian women too such as Elizabeth Arden, Gail Cook-Bennett, Flora McCrae Eaton, Elisabeth Bruyere, Kathleen E. Sendall, Dr. Roberta Bondar, Kate Aitken, Dr Ruth Marion Bell, Ojibwa Elsie Knott, Margaret Atwood,

Barbara Ann Scott, Judge Emily Murphy and of course our current Governor General, Her Excellency the Right Honourable Michaëlle Jean. The list continues.

The world of entertainment is also proud of the outstanding achievements of Sarah McLachlan, Anne Murray, K.D. Lang, Shania Twain and Celine Dion and many others.

In some ways, Barbara Harmer's story of a woman struggling for recognition of purpose and breaking new ground in a man's world is typical of them all. Now, women in senior positions around the globe stand as beacons to girls and young women everywhere who have that glint of ambition in their eye and a burning feeling for achievement in their heart.

There should be no barrier to prevent any woman to achieve their potential after having been downtrodden for centuries. Times are definitely -a-changing and all humanity is benefiting as a result. There seem to be no bounds now and even the skies are no longer the limits.

Today, daughters everywhere are being told, "Go for it. Set your goals, believe in yourself, have confidence in your ability; work hard at developing a skill and the world really can be your oyster."

"You live in exciting times, take advantage of the many opportunities afforded to you and grab the brass ring."

And save for your retirement. But you must start NOW!

IMPULSE BUYING – are you spending your retirement fund?

One of the most pleasant ways for many women to spend their time is to wander through a quality shopping arcade, viewing all of the merchandise on show and for the moment, imagining that they can have just about anything that catches their eye. Is that you perhaps? The key word here of course is *"imagine"*. In reality, with a credit card in your pocket, you just know that you CAN have almost anything that catches your eye but the danger that lurks is that at some point, perhaps this year or maybe next year, the amount shown on the price tag must be paid and it will come right out of your bank account.

But for the moment, suppose that you really do like the pair of shoes that you see and you are convincing yourself that they are exactly the colour that you need. The cost on the underside of the sole tells you that they normally sell for $249.99. As you study the label you notice the red line crossing through the original price and that the revised price is $195.99. But wait a moment! You glance again and see that this too is struck through with another red line and now, today, these "must-have" shoes are on sale for the unbelievably low price of $149.95.

IMPORTANT POINT

ARE YOUR PENSION FUND PAYMENTS

GOING INTO THE RIGHT ACCOUNT?

Here immediately blossoms an instant love affair between you and the shoes and a quick calculation tells you that there is a savings to be made in the amount of one hundred dollars if you buy them today. And that is a lot of money to save in anyone's book. And aren't you regularly encouraged to save?

You tell yourself that not only will you be one hundred dollars better off if you buy these shoes today, but in addition, they really are the colour you have been looking for. And the style is just like you have seen in all of the ads this year – these have just got to be the season's latest - direct from Europe.

As you try them on you can almost hear your friends and work colleagues ooing and aring with envy at these very expensive shoes and of course, they will never know that you got them on sale.

"Yes, I'll take these please," you say as the store assistant stands waiting for you to make your decision. As you spoke you felt that there were eyes watching and ears waiting for your decision. You felt unbelievably important as you spoke to the assistant and authorised an expensive purchase as if it was an everyday occurrence.

"Thank you ma'am, would you like them in a box or in a bag?"

A picture flashes through your mind. It is of you, travelling home impressing other shoppers with the large designer bag. The decision is made.

"A bag will be fine." You try to remain calm wanting to confirm the illusion that you pay this price for shoes almost every day of your life.

As you arrive at the counter the assistant asks, "Will that be cash or charge Ma'am?"

You know all the time what the answer will be but you want the charade to continue. "Er, perhaps I'll charge it. Yes. I can use the extra air miles." As if for you, there was any other choice. Your credit card is already well over its limit.

As you leave the store and stroll through the fashionable part of town there is a wonderful feeling of self-importance, and why not. You work very hard for your boss. Your designer bag announces to the world that you can afford to shop in one of the most exclusive stores in town and only you know your secret, that in fact, your credit card is over its maximum allowance and that these shoes will probably not be paid for until a few years down the road.

But the feeling you experience from the scenario is exciting and provides you with a distinct buzz, almost like a drug – you have had your fix for now and you are content – until the next time.

You tell yourself the cost was really worth it and what the heck, life is short anyway and you probably won't always look this good and so the transaction was certainly justified. And in any event, you don't do this sort of thing every day. "Just as well," you muse to yourself as you swagger along the wide tree-lined shopping avenue with an air of confidence, knowing that the shoes will add to your overall attractiveness.

A few weeks later, it is a Saturday and you are downtown with a good friend looking for nothing in particular but enjoying the bright sunny day in a nice part of the city.

"Oh look," announces your friend as she peers through a large store window. "That top is exactly what I am looking for to go with a pair of pants I bought last week."

As your friend is trying on the top, you find yourself browsing through the rails of clothes and surprise, surprise, here is a business suit that goes exactly with that snazzy pair of shoes you bought last month.

You try it on.

You look a million dollars.

You make the purchase.

"Will that be cash or charge Ma'am?"

"Er, Charge please" you reply, as you hand over your well-worn credit card. Once again you have a nice designer bag to impress other shoppers and again, you go through the usual excuses in your mind to substantiate the purchase.

And so it goes on, impulsive shopping. Week after week, month after month and you just love it.

Now I am not the sort of person to pour rain on your parade and if you feel that this is a sensible way to invest your money then fine, go ahead, especially if you have shares in the shoe company. But be warned. When you wake up one morning and find that you are seventy, because at some point you will, you'll likely have many regrets as you live in poverty and you will very much resent that Robert Kite and his wife lived out their retirement years in glorious comfort while you will be getting used to being nearly destitute.

Look! I really want to earnestly persuade you that this sort of impulsive spending just has to stop. NOW! I'm sure that the shoes look great. And you look fabulous in the business suit. But you don't need me to tell you that you already have lots of clothes in the closet at home. In fact, if you are honest with yourself, you may even need to pitch some of them out so as to make room for the new ones. Polly does that all the time I think.

And as for shoes, how many pairs of feet do you have for goodness sake? And what's all this about designer bags just to impress lots of other shoppers and travellers that you don't even know. Who cares what they think, and anyway, they probably don't envy you one bit. They maybe even think how stupid you are to pay up-town prices for goods that you can get elsewhere for a fraction of the cost.

Just for a moment, I want you to think about that scenario while I conduct a simple exercise. I want you to think about that pair of shoes - that expensive pair of shoes that we just discussed. Next, I want you to take a look at the FINANCIAL CHART headed Impulse Buying Substitute that is included in this chapter.

Let us imagine, just for a second that you repeat this shopping spree seven or eight times each year. Of course, I realise that you don't but just for the sake of the exercise, let us imagine that you do. Now, I want you to multiply the price of the pair of shoes, which was $149.95 by the number eight. I think that without adding any provincial or federal taxes the calculation total is within a few cents of $1,200.

Next, I want you to believe for a moment that when you first saw the shoes, you actually saw your pension fund. You naturally exercised great self-discipline and said no to the shoes. In fact, you said "No!" eight times that first year. How much will you have in your pocket? I think it should be about $1,200.

Now, take the $1,200 to a trusting fund manager and put it in an investment fund. With moderate risk you will watch it grow by about ten percent each year. In addition, you will repeat the exercise next year, and the next year and so on for a total of twenty-years, after which period of time you will have spent $24,000. But not on impulse shopping but rather on an investment that will help to give you a comfortable retirement.

(Don't forget that to have $24,000 to spend, you will need to earn about $29,000 and then pay the government $5,000 in income tax. That leaves you with the $24,000).

But we haven't finished yet.

You will put away $24,000 over 20 years and as a reward for using your money, you will receive interest of $41,000.

And so your total nest egg in your account will be over $65,000 – after just 20 years.

But that's still not quite the end of the exercise. There's more yet. If you choose to leave your total prize untouched for a further 10-years, without adding anything to it, at 10% per annum it will grow to $169,000. Not bad.

However, as instead, you chose to buy the shoes let's now examine the real cost of your decision. Firstly, you threw away the opportunity to lend someone $100 each month for a period of 20-years for which you would have received the handsome prize of $41,000. That is the amount of interest that the investment would have earned you.

Next, you recall that the reduced price asked for the shoes was $149.95. If you lived in Ontario you would pay Federal tax and Provincial tax which brings the retail price of the shoes to about $171.

Then, you chose to charge them to your credit card, knowing that the sum of $171 would probably stay unpaid for longer than a year, and in fact, as money was tight for you during the next few years you could afford to pay only the minimum payment on your credit card monthly statement.

As a result, you will pay interest for each year in the amount of say 23% and after 3 years, if you still have an outstanding balance on your statement exceeding $171 and in theory, your shoes remained as part of the outstanding balance; you will pay a total of $318 for the shoes that had a bargain tag price of $149.95.

The point that I make once more, is that most everyone has sufficient money during their life to provide them with a comfortable retirement. The difficulty for me is trying to convince them or in this case, YOU, to spend wisely on things that you really *need* (such as a Retirement Plan) rather than to purchase unnecessary things on an impulse. As they say, you pay now or you WILL pay later.

HAVE I LEFT IT TOO LATE – the options for late starters
Guys – You can stay with this one too, especially if you also are a late starter.

If you are a late starter then both you and I have a lot in common for I was that person too. But it turned out o.k. With the help and co-operation of Polly, we exercised major self-discipline big time. We severely restricted our spending habits, we stayed focused on the major objective (which was to be debt free at sixty-five) and we

maximised our investment opportunities by frequently monitoring
the fund values and ensuring that our investments were well diversified.

Also, Polly would regularly sign up for new credit cards
offering a really low interest rate and then, transfer any unpaid balance
so as to capitalize on the opportunity.

IMPORTANT POINT

EARLY BIRDS AND LATE STARTERS
CAN SHARE THE SAME DREAM

PREPARE YOUR RETIREMENT PLAN
AS EARLY AS POSSIBLE

BUT IT IS NEVER TOO LATE!

All of these practices are fine however if your age is under 50.
If you are over fifty then you are what I would call a late, late starter.
But do not despair. There is hope for you as there is hope for everyone.
We are all living longer and so as you may live until you are 95, you
need to prepare a retirement or financial plan that will take you through
the next 30 years or so.

There is no point in being resentful or regretful because you
didn't save and invest when you should have done. There is no point in
being angry with your spouse or partner thinking that they were the one
who should have seen this mess approaching and made some decision
to avoid it. You cannot change the past but you can prepare for your
future and the easiest way to do that is to start with a large sheet of
paper and start right NOW. Prepare yourself a Retirement Plan.

Anyone can do it and I repeat that it is never too late.

There is no secret to building yourself a large nest egg, but you
must be self-disciplined. If you have left it late in the day to start your
Retirement Plan then spend your money with your investment advisor -

not in the stores and remember perhaps most of all, *diversify your investments*. As my dear Mother used to tell me, "Robert, never put all of your eggs in one basket."

Chapter Four
WHERE AM I NOW?
How to assess my current worth?

"Where am I now?" We are talking about finances of course and the whole point of the question is to get you to focus your mind at this point in time on your major assets. The valuable ones - you know, the objects that you personally own and the things that have some real value such as your bank account and your savings account, your investments including any RRSPs and any tangible assets that you own such as a house, a car, a boat, and perhaps if you are lucky, a cottage.

You may have some expensive jewellery, valuable furniture or paintings. This is the time to consider their value too. Of course, if you are anything like me it is likely that some of your possessions will not immediately spring to mind especially if you have a house that you have lived in for many years. Things just accumulate and often get lost somewhere, probably in the basement if you don't get down there very often.

I want to explain to you how to set up a financial grid so as to assess your current net worth as it is that figure that will form the foundation for your future nest egg. You will need to take this seriously and be very thorough in your homework.

Take a few moments and give some thought to what things you might have and want to include in your list. There may be a battered old box containing a stamp collection or some old coins or you might have an old vase that an aunt or uncle gave you some years ago that you thought was fit for the trash can.

It could just be that these sorts of trinkets are worth more than you think and so you should certainly give some time to consider their value or seek professional help if necessary. Less valuable things such as the kitchen appliances and general house furniture need not be included.

I want you to be in the position to assess your *total* current worth so of course, that will include everything and although perhaps a bit daunting at first, you will find this task very interesting I promise you. The process will actually force you to consider the matter very thoroughly indeed, because when we get to the relevant part later in the chapter, you will need to be in a position to fairly and truthfully place a current value on each item.

How about that old toy that you have kept since you were a child or a doll or a game that is still in its original packaging, albeit somewhat tatty after so many years of neglect. These sorts of oddments are fetching fortunes these days and so that is another reason why it is especially important to jot down a list of all of the things that you can think of that has any value at all.

Actually, this might be a good time to take a look at the reference sheet that I have included with the book to help you compile your list of current assets and their values in an orderly fashion. It is the one headed *PERSONAL NET WORTH ASSESSMENT REGISTER*.

If you live with another then you will need absolute co-operation from your spouse or partner and you should both be like-minded. If you live by yourself then you are in complete control and in some ways, it might be easier.

O.K. Let's get started. Let's begin first by you finding a quiet area of the house where you can work undisturbed. You should have a large writing pad, a calculator and a pen or pencil as well as a clear space on a large table. This way you can better organise your documentation file as you build it.

Whatever your age, in order that you can properly prepare your Retirement Plan you need to first record some personal data regarding your finances and in this regard, you may find some of the charts that I have included to be useful working tools. They have helped me enormously over the years and so I know that they work. You should find that they assist you too by more easily grouping together amounts of money and numbers in sensible clusters. This will keep things tidy and in an easy-to-read format.

You will notice that the chart or grid contains lots of squares organised in columns and rows. The numbers that you find already in these squares or fields are only examples and these should be ignored. Delete or erase them if you wish.

Start by copying the chart and filling in the boxes that make up the column on the left. I have provided some suggestions such as Real Estate, Investments, Savings and other personal assets.

Next, it is a good idea to give a description of the item and you can do this in the next column. The third column is for the current estimated value and while this does not need to be absolutely accurate, you should get as near to the true value as possible. Don't worry about the odd cents. Round everything to the nearest dollar. Remember, the results of your work here will form the foundation for your nest egg.

The next column exists to identify any debt that you might have against the item. As the objective of this exercise is to identify the true net value of your assets, it is important that you enter any money that you owe against the item. Otherwise the value of the item will be accurate but your personal asset value will not be.

So, if you own a house that has a market value of $450,000 and you have a mortgage of $200,000, the true net asset value is calculated at $250,000, and so on down the page.

IMPORTANT POINT

DO NOT OVERVALUE YOUR ASSETS

When all the spaces have been filled you will easily find your TOTAL NET WORTH. This is in fact the total value of your assets less any money you owe.

Congratulations! If you have never completed this procedure before then perhaps you didn't realise that you were worth as much as you are.

This is probably a good time to gather some other information that you should have close to hand as you work your way through the preparation of your Retirement Plan.

You already have a list of Personal Assets and a list of your Personal Debts but how about your Monthly Income and Expenditure streams? If you don't remember exactly how much you earn each month don't worry, you won't be alone. But these numbers will be important to your work and so take a look around for recent bank statements or pay stubs and keep these together with other important personal financial information.

Did I mention expenditures? Most people have no idea how much they spend each month. They just know that their pay goes into their bank account and that they pay any bills that come in out of the same account. If there is any left then great but that is not a common occurrence these days.

It is good to have an idea as to what you spend if you are to take this project seriously. How will you know if you are cutting down on your monthly spending if you have no spend totals to guide you?

I've included a grid for you to easily monitor your monthly spend. It is titled MONTHLY BUDGET – LIVING COSTS. Take a look at it and see if the items in it are familiar to you. Perhaps you can copy the main structure of it and adapt it to your personal use. It worked well for me, and so with a few minor changes it should work well for you too.

The exercise that we have just gone through together should have identified to you the following important statistics.

        i.Personal Assets
        ii.Personal debts
        iii.Personal Income
        iv.Personal Expenditures

Familiar knowledge of these four areas of your finance is very critical to you as you work your way through the years of your Retirement Plan towards your retirement. This collective information will tell you where you are now, financially speaking. It will also announce to you how much you earned last month and how much you spent last month.

That is the monthly data you need to calculate how much of your monthly income is surplus at the end of every month. And when you add the surplus to your revised personal assets you then have the complete picture.

Make no mistake. I cannot overstate that this part of your homework is very critical if your Retirement Plan is to be successful. You cannot afford to be casual about collecting this monthly information and monitoring it well enough to understand it. If your particular ship is to sail a well-charted course and arrive safely at it's destination port, like any successful navigator you will need to know where you are at any given point in time. It's a big ocean out there with some mighty icebergs and dangerous rocks, as well as the odd shark nosing around to pick up unnoticed assets that fall overboard.

Those assets might be yours and they may well be valuable.

You are now at the helm of this vessel and the success of this voyage will very much depend on you!

Next. You need to agree on your Fund Manager because he or she will be a major component in your strategy. If you have any doubts or need any ideas then read the chapter titled *Investment Advisor – How can I pick a good one?*

A fund manager and an investment advisor can be the same person because your investment advisor will usually be managing your funds. It is best that way so that you need to deal with only one person.

Now, take a break and catch your breath and when you come back you will need to think about making some major decisions regarding how much you can safely save every month. There must be some small change rattling around somewhere that is superfluous. We need to harness that small asset and invest it wisely so as to make it grow. Every dollar saved now will add to the nest egg that you so dearly want in your future. You can do it - But you must start NOW!

MONTHLY SAVINGS WILL UNDERPIN YOUR RETIREMENT PLAN.

Remember, we are told by the experts that for every five-years that you delay saving for your retirement days, you will need to double the amount of your contributions for your fund to have the same value. So, if when you were 35 years old you were told that to have a decent pension you would need to save $250 each month, at 40 years old you will need to save $500 each month to enjoy the same pension fund and so on. At 45 years old, $1,000 and at 50 years old you will need to save $2,000 every month to achieve the same fund value. Suddenly, $250 a-month seems like a bargain and don't you wish you were 35 again?

If you are convinced that the experts are right in what they say, or even partly right, you don't need me to preach any more on this subject. Except I will say, that you do not need to delay your plan for 5-years to miss out. Just substitute the word "year" for "month" and the answers come out just the same. And remember. You can never go back, so take a good look in the darkest recesses of your pocket book and see if you can manage to put away a few extra dollars each month towards your nest egg. You won't regret it I promise you.

Have you given any thought as to how much you should have saved so as to make it possible for you to retire? The magic figure? In my case there was not so much as a magic figure as the need to be debt free. I knew that I would have some pensions dribbling in my direction each month and so long as my living costs were low then a savings account would be there to act as an emergency fund. In case Polly or I needed costly home care.

If you are still working however, and notwithstanding any company pension fund you may be contributing to, then a magic figure might be the amount of money that you need to save every month so as to build a retirement savings fund sufficient to feed any emergency need that you may have in your particular circumstance.

Whatever your circumstance, what is the magic figure for you? What is the amount that you need to save each month to ensure that dream retirement? Perhaps you already have some savings and maybe you also have that company pension plan with the firm that you work for. If so then the future for you may look very good. But will it be sufficient? You cannot have too much and so by using some of the formulae in this book, you should calculate the magic figure that will work for you.

Personally, I find that it is best if you can do this *without* the input of your fund manager. You need to be able to change your mind freely. Meanwhile, a professional person present may create an added stress level that you can do without and you might feel pressured to make a decision in their presence and regret it afterwards.

There will be enough time later when their input will be helpful if not vital so as to build you a nice investment fund that they will manage on your behalf.

But now, you need to identify exactly how much you can put aside each month to invest into your Retirement Plan. This is the protocol. These are the procedures you could follow.

Carefully examine your monthly costs and strip out anything and everything that you can safely get by without.

Consider making major changes to your lifestyle if necessary such as downsizing your house, especially if you have a large mortgage. Even if you have a small mortgage, a downsize may erase the need for any mortgage whatsoever. This could save you hundreds of dollars each month, creating excess dollars that can form the base of your investment fund.

If you have two cars, consider managing with just one car. These are the sorts of tough decisions and self-constraint that you need to impose upon yourself now if you are to succeed in achieving that retirement dream down the road. But you need to start NOW!

IMPORTANT POINT

NONE OF US HAS A CRYSTAL BALL

EARN AND SAVE NOW

WHILE YOU ARE HEALTHY AND ABLE

Now that you have trimmed down your monthly costs, identify the amount of money that you feel you can safely give to your fund manager each month, making sure that you retain sufficient for all of your needs and perhaps a little more for emergencies.

Remember, if you are healthy and working at this time, then these are definitely the days to start saving big time for your retirement. You may be ill and jobless in the future and then you won't have any spare money available to save for your retirement.

Sleep on the decision for a day or two and at some point after that, if you feel sure that you have considered all of the options, then make an appointment to visit your fund manager or financial advisor to discuss your requirements. If you don't have a fund manager then you could start by asking to see the investment manager at your local bank. They are extremely helpful and usually quite knowledgeable.

IMPORTANT POINT

BEFORE YOU GO INTO A MEETING

PREPARE A LIST -

MAKE SURE YOU KNOW WHAT

YOU WANT TO COME OUT WITH!

There are several charts in this book that serve as examples to show you how much your investment can grow by putting aside monthly amounts. You could use these as guidelines, but I stress that they are examples and are provided for you to use as helpful guidelines only.

Your personal experience will of course be different from mine and remember to always be sure to discuss everything necessary with your professional advisor so that you fully understand what you are getting into.

Remember, it is *your* money and many people much smarter than you or I have made big mistakes, only to see their investments disappear, mainly, by not being diversified, being too trusting of their financial managers and the system or not doing their homework.

Your investment advisor can only do so much for you and so it is *your* responsibility to regularly monitor your savings and immediately speak to your advisor if you feel anything is not right. To delay could cost you dearly. If the thought comes to your mind that there might be something wrong, there probably is.

IMPORTANT POINT

INVESTMENTS AND SAVINGS -

DIVERSIFICATION <u>IS</u>

THE NAME OF THE GAME

Remember, some types of investments can go down as well as up. Get to know which are the high-risk investments and use these only if you completely understand how they work and more importantly, that you feel comfortable with the higher level of risk that you will be undertaking. High-risk investments are not for the faint hearted. Neither are they for the short-term investor.

The attraction that is associated with high risk investments is the higher levels of interest that they yield and so if someone advises you that that you can get a return on your money of say 25% per year for an investment period of 3-years in a sector such as industrial real estate or natural gas exploration, then open your ears, listen up, and allow your senses to tell you that with a high yield comes a high risk. Let caution be your byword.

After you have read the prospectus that accompanies the fund on offer, you may still wish to invest in the fund. O.K. But if the risk seems higher than you are used to, then I suggest that you invest only an amount of money that you can afford to lose. Over the long term such as 25-years, the investment might be fine because you have the years when it may bounce back, but be aware of the risks. Differentiate between investing and gambling. There is a big difference.

Assuming that you are starting to prepare your Retirement Plan now, next year, on the first anniversary date of your Retirement Plan, you will need to assess your total worth all over again. But don't worry, the second time is always easier because you know what to expect and the cost of living index will be a useful basic guideline for you to use.

The reason for conducting this exercise each year is to determine with a high degree of accuracy the annual growth of your assets; assets that you will depend on to provide you with your dreams in your retirement years. If you inflate the value of your assets in any way this year, when you sit down to measure the growth of your assets next year, you will be looking at a distorted set of figures in terms of asset growth and you will be very disappointed with the results.

Also, if you are not using accurate figures (or as near accurate as you can determine) in *any* part of your Retirement Plan, then your long-range financial forecasts will be wrong and the result will be that your projected pension numbers will also be wrong. Honesty is the name of the game and the success of your Retirement Plan will very much depend on you and how you prepare and manage the Plan. Remember, *you* are the project manager and as with any major undertaking the results will very much depend on preparation, thoroughness, consistency and supreme management of the project to its very end.

So in a nutshell, the object of the exercise here is to record truthful information only because if this part is wrong, then so will be your projected numbers. The disastrous results will be that your retirement dreams will have insufficient funds to underpin their success. But enough of the future, let's get back to the spreadsheets.

The real estate values should be fairly easy to assess but again, take the time to be as near accurate as possible. A discrepancy of ten thousand dollars at this stage could convert into errors of hundreds of thousands of dollars down the road in say, twenty-five years.

The car and boat estimates should be fairly easy too. But when you get to the lines where you have savings, stocks and shares and pension investments, well, you may need to make some 'phone calls or seek professional help.

The section with antiques and paintings, furniture, jewellery etc., may be a bit difficult too but again, if you estimate the values as accurately as you can then it should be fine.

By now, you will have totalled the numbers in the Estimated Values column and at the bottom of the column you will see the true value of your Total Worth. Except remember that this is a *gross* value because it is likely that you do not own outright some of the items such as the house or the car. You need to deduct the outstanding amounts that you owe on each line item including any money outstanding on a credit card etc., from the *gross* values. That is the purpose of the next column headed Current Debt Owing.

Now take a moment to reflect upon what you have done and the figures that you have entered on the work sheet. In the example that I have provided in the book you will see that the amount of the debt is about two hundred thousand dollars *less* than the net worth and so, without the debt, the owner of this Retirement Plan would in fact have a Personal Total Net Worth of an amount of money in excess of one million, one hundred thousand dollars.

IMPORTANT POINT

DEBT FREE AT 65 IS NOT AN OPTION

Next, take another look at your own Net Worth Register in its completed form. Is there anything that you would change if you could? It is probably the column that contains your debt. Right? Well, it is hoped that a regular look at this spreadsheet will motivate you to erase any debt as soon as possible and start *earning* interest instead of *paying* it. Perhaps now, you can see how important it is for you to be <u>debt free at 65</u>.

As mentioned earlier, so that you can monitor the growth in your personal wealth, which in time will become your retirement nest egg, every year you will need to re-assess the value of your assets.

Similarly, you will be required to make an annual estimate of the financial value of the contents in your home. You will need to do this for the company that you have your home and contents insured with. Maybe that would be an excellent time to review all of your assets and liabilities and so carry out the two tasks at the same time.

YOUR MONEY MAY BE SAFE – DOES IT KNOW WHERE YOU ARE?

The exact process for conducting the exercise described in this chapter will likely be similar for everyone but of course the details will vary somewhat and in some cases may very considerably. For example, if you have lived a stable sort of a life remaining in one town or city or have stayed in one job for a long time then your work will be simplified. You won't need to do too much delving to establish the value of your property and the value of your savings and investments.

But if you have been employed in a job that has caused you to relocate to work in several cities or even different countries, then there may be numerous bank accounts, and even perhaps more than one property. If you are in this situation then to calculate your full worth may take a little more time, especially if you haven't assessed the value of your assets recently.

Even without a Retirement Plan you may feel that it is a useful idea to conduct an annual assessment of your net worth - perhaps at the end of each year during the few days when some of us get a break from work during the holiday season running up to New Year.

If you have been spending some of your working life living in a foreign country, then the exchange rates between foreign currencies alone can create a major swing in your wealth, particularly if your assets are considerable. Moreover, as the major banks and financial institutions increasingly merge or find themselves being taken over, it can be quite a task to find out who even owns the fund where you may keep some of your savings. And here's a thought. Do the fund holders really know where *you* are?

My friend Martin and his lovely wife Corinne were both from South Africa originally and met when they were working in a hospital in London, U.K. Recently, they received a large envelope in the mail, apparently from a small bank in England, the sort of bank that specializes in mortgage loans and is called a building society.

The envelope contained a notice of a future Annual General Meeting and interestingly, they were encouraged to vote for the election of some of the directors and other agenda motions on-line via their internet website. Seemingly, they found this quite useful as it was economical and time-efficient, because after all, they weren't going to travel to the U.K. for this purpose alone. And of course, it saved them the cost of the postage.

Corinne then called her friend Alan who had also worked in the U.K. some years ago. She knew that he also had maintained a small savings account with the same institution.

"Hi Alan," she said. "Have you received a letter inviting you to the meeting of the building society?"

"No, I haven't" he replied. "What is the meeting about?"

She told him that it was the usual annual general meeting stuff with the same old agenda of electing directors, auditors, and setting directors' bonuses. Actually, some of these items can be quite important at times and so she encouraged him to look through the contents of the envelope.

IMPORTANT POINT

ALWAYS STAY IN TOUCH

The interesting point here is that Alan hadn't advised the building society of his change of address. While this in itself was not a good idea and perhaps an oversight when he moved to Canada, the more serious point is that in the U. K., building societies are considered in law, to be "owned" by the members of the society – the savers and investors like you and me. The rules can change from time to time of course, but to qualify as a full member you merely need to open an account with a particular minimum balance.

If at some future point-in-time, the directors and members have a vote to become a public company, then all of the members would receive shares in the new publicly listed company, which could be quite valuable. The shares would be registered and listed on the London Stock Exchange.

The new owners would have an option of electing to either sell these shares or to keep them. Thus, Alan, by failing to provide his new address, could miss out on a windfall of several thousands of dollars, particularly if he forgot about them for the long term.

While this scenario may sound doubtful, financial institutions tell me that the number of customers who fail to provide them with a current address is considerable. So don't forget, always stay in touch. Always ensure that any bank or other financial institution that you deal with is notified of any change of address, telephone number or any other contact details. In fact, it is a good idea every few years to drop them a line to provide them with an update. It is in your own interest. After all, we are talking here of a large part of your life savings.

HAVE YOU SET YOUR RETIREMENT AGE?

At some point in the future you may want to consider exactly the time when you want to retire from full time employment. At that time you will need to know something about your finances. Correction! You will need to know EVERYTHING about your finances. The trouble is, when we are working full time, it is the job and the associated worries that occupies our minds most. Unfortunately this leaves little or no time to give any serious thought to our finances. This dilemma can be quite dangerous in fact, for at any time, without expecting it, we may be rushed into making a financially related decision in a hurry without having complete knowledge of the details.

All decisions concerning our finances deserve our full attention. We need as much time as is necessary to think things through. Even the smallest detail today may grow into a major problem tomorrow if not acted on with full consideration for all of the ramifications and possibilities.

In the legal profession there is an expression that is used to underscore the importance of time. *Time is of the Essence.* Strictly speaking it is a phrase that is often used in contracts which in effect says, *"The specified time and dates in this agreement are vital and thus mandatory, and "we mean it." Therefore any delay, reasonable or not, slight or not, will be grounds for cancelling the agreement."*

The important thing when it comes to dealing with your personal finances is to consider all aspects of the matter and decide in your own time. Few things are more important than your personal finances and isn't it true that we can usually find time for anything that we think is important?

This brings to mind a situation that occurred to me many years ago and one that I have never forgotten. I was in my teens at home alone. It was during the late morning and I was on summer holidays from school when there was a knock on the front door. I was just finishing showering and so I quickly threw some clothes on and dashed down the stairs.

I opened the door and was temporary blinded by the bright sunlight. After a second or two I made out the silhouette of a man and a woman. They were total strangers, smartly dressed and both carried brief cases.

"Are your parents in?" the woman asked.

"No, I'm afraid not" I replied.

"Well, perhaps *you* might be interested in what we have to say," they added, directing their attention to me.

I made an attempt to appear interested in their conversation – which actually wasn't too difficult because as I recall it, I found the woman to be very attractive.

They asked if I went to church and then launched into their presentation about their particular religious viewpoint. After about five-minutes or so, they began to leave and as they did so the woman turned back to face me and added,

"You may not realize this now, but as we all set aside enough time to have meals three-times a-day, so in the future, we will all set aside specific times to devote to religious studies each day." She smiled as she said "Good bye" and thanked me for my time.

"Good bye" I stammered, as her final words lingered in the late morning mist. They walked down the garden path under the lilac trees, opened the gate and let themselves out. I never saw either of them again.

That lady will never know the impact that her final statement had on me. I found that comment pretty powerful stuff. Perhaps it was because I was a young lad and was eager to learn about life. At that time anything new that I had not heard before remained with me until I understood it thoroughly. Anyway, what she said had a great effect on me to the point that I have never forgotten it. Not so the religious content, but the final statement itself.

I thought it through constantly for many days until I was able to make sense of the complete meaning or at least, what her comment meant to me. This is what I learned on that day:

That I would always find time to do the things in life that were important to me. Period!

Pretty basic stuff you might say and you are right.

And so, coming back to the question, "Where am I now?" If we don't know where we are, with, for example our finances, what does that say?

It should tell you that your finances are thought to be pretty low on your list of priorities in life but more importantly, that if you are expecting to make a decision regarding retirement somewhere down the road then you had better review your prioritizing skills and know exactly what total assets you have, where your savings are invested, the amount of annual return and the level of risk to your investments.

So where are you now? Well, you may have completed a spreadsheet or two and discovered your total net worth, but there are a number of other important factors that you need to consider. For ease of reference, I will include them in this chapter.

The place where you live - do you own or rent it?

Do you make regular payments into an RRSP account for yourself? Or another?

Are you married or single?

Do you have children?

Is there any chance that you will be expected to support parents, siblings or others while you are working or when you retire?

Where are your R. R. S. P.'s or other savings invested?

Is your money working hard enough for you, given the level of risk that you can tolerate?

These details are all factors that we need to consider in the Retirement Plan. The answers to these questions could have a dynamic effect on the long-term shape of the plan and so it is important that we know the answers and record them here.

Next. Let's assume that you are in the first year of your Retirement Plan and that you are in your early forties. Assume that within fifteen years you are likely to become an empty nester.

You currently still have a mortgage. But you have already memorized the key phrase to the Retirement Plan.

I will be debt free when I am 65.

That is where you want to be. That is your goal and it should never vary.

So! You need a future Retirement Plan that will take you there - A future Retirement Plan that will take you to the year in which you will be 65.

Remember, this will be the year in which you will make the final payment of your mortgage.

To be DEBT FREE when you are 65 will be critical for several reasons.

The lower your income, the less income tax you will need to pay.

A monthly mortgage or car payment will cause you to need to receive *more* income. This could take you onto a higher tax level.

A continuing mortgage or car payment could erase that winter-cruise in the sun.

RETIREES PAY INCOME TAX. Why use part of your pension to pay tax when it could go towards funding your retirement dream. Why risk letting your dream turn into a nightmare?

IMPORTANT POINT

EXTRA MORTGAGE PAYMENTS

ARE LIKE FERTILIZER

During your working years you have lots of money to spend. I know, because I see it every time I visit shopping malls. People everywhere are busy spending money on all sorts of items - most of them unnecessary. Often, I turn to Polly and say,

"Look Polly, look at all those people spending their retirement pension on useless things that they don't really need."

It makes me think that almost everyone can afford a decent pension but instead of making payments to their Retirement Plan they are deciding to spend it on unnecessary items. That is another reason for me to write this book. You probably have a decent pension but you are spending it now before you retire! There will be nothing left for you at 65 and so there will be no retirement dreams for you.

Listen. I am now going to make a suggestion to you that if followed, will save you many thousands of dollars.

If you agree that perhaps you do spend some money each week that you could save then here's the plan. I know it works because I have used it and it saved Polly and me many thousands of dollars.

How much do you think you could save each week by improving your spending habits? Could it be fifty dollars each week? O.K. But I am going to give you a break and halve it, so the actual amount that you pledge to put aside each week will be $25.00.

In 12-months time you will have saved $1,300.

If you pay down that amount each year of a twenty-five year mortgage you will make extra payments of $32,500 but it doesn't finish there. The extra mortgage payments annually in the amount of $1,300 will save you many thousands of extra dollars. It's true – speak to your bank officer.

IMPORTANT POINT

EXTRA MORTGAGE PAYMENTS

MAKE YOUR MONEY TREE

GROW!!!

Amazing isn't it and all for twenty-five dollars a week. You see? You really are richer than you think. But perhaps you would prefer an alternative suggestion. Then how about this one?

AT THE END OF EACH YEAR, MAKE AN EXTRA PAYMENT TO YOUR MORTGAGE ACCOUNT EQUAL TO AT LEAST ONE MONTH OF YOUR MORTGAGE PAYMENT. TWO MONTHS IF YOU CAN AFFORD IT.

Usually, you must make this arrangement possible by negotiating this point when setting up your mortgage but in any event, it may not be too late. Discuss it with your mortgagor or bank officer. Also, be sure that they agree to adjust the mortgage immediately after the payment is made. That way you will benefit from the interest that you will save.

Let me show you how you could save some more money from your everyday costs and help make this simple step a reality. (You've probably heard this before, but if so, then why are you still buying coffee every day?)

Let us say that you spend two dollars on a morning coffee on the way to work each day, perhaps an unnecessary cup of coffee! Okay! Presuming that you work a 48-week year. That is $480.00 that you could use to pay down some of your mortgage each year! In five years you have spent $2,400. If you are now 45, by the time you are 65 you will have spent $9,600.00!! Was the coffee really that good?

By the way, don't forget to add interest to the $9,600 that you would have saved had you used this "coffee money" to pay down more of your mortgage each year!

Let's try something else. Maybe you smoke? There are some people who still do. At around five bucks a pack, if you smoke a pack a day then each year you are setting fire to $1,825. If you paid that off your mortgage every year for twenty-years that would amount to an extra $36,500 coming directly off the principal. My local mortgage specialist tells me that this sort of annual payment would save thousands of dollars in interest over the lifetime of a mortgage. In addition, the mortgage could be paid off a few years earlier. Just imagine, no mortgage left to pay by the time you get to aged sixty-one.

Have I got your attention yet? Well, how about this one?

Do you happen to have a mortgage of around $150,000.00? If it is a fixed rate of 5% and the term is 25 years, the monthly payments will be a little under $900.00 each month.

The <u>Interest</u> that you will pay over the life of the mortgage will be about:

$113,066.00

That's just the Interest! That is what you are paying for the privilege of borrowing the money.

Wouldn't you want to pay that off as soon as possible and save some money?

You may be surprised at how much you can save yourself by paying that extra few hundred dollars or so every year. Remember, we are talking here of serious savings, and it is all tax-free!

At 45, you may feel that retirement is too far off and that the present time is the time when you should be enjoying yourself. "Why not?" you ask yourself.

"I might not even live to see 65 and so why go through all this pain and strain?"

Let me tell you something. Much of the pain and strain probably comes from having big financial debts and the worry that goes with them.

Also, with today's wonderful medical science the odds are that you will live for a very long time. You are very likely to survive well past the retirement age and perhaps even into your nineties. Imagine, living from 65 to 90 on the breadline!

Twenty-five years spent just watching your friends enjoying winter cruises and trips to Europe and Florida every winter while you are left at home to shovel snow or wait for the swallows to return!

No! The risk is not worth it.

Again, I urge you to make a decision now to prepare your personal Retirement Plan so that your mortgage will have a good chance to be fully paid off. In addition, there could well be sufficient pensions and savings that will give you and your spouse the fun and the financial freedom that you long for and that you deserve. If you like the sound of this, then read on. We have only just begun!

Chapter Five
FINANCIAL PLANS
Are they smoke and mirrors?

WHAT CONSTITUTES A FINANCIAL PLAN?

I thought that perhaps it would be a good idea to discuss financial plans at some stage in the book because almost everyone handles them at some time or another. Also, during my lifetime I have noticed that many of us often underestimate the *true value* of financial plans especially when they present themselves as a grid of figures or masquerade as an important document, when all the time we know them to be a piece of promotional literature hoping to entice us to part with our money. Promotions for this or that and invitations to apply for a credit card or for some get-rich investment scheme.

Financial Plans come in many shapes, sizes and disguises. For example, the statements that you receive each month from suppliers of services that you buy are a type of financial plan in that they contain useful financial information set down in different ways and some of these if used properly can help you to budget for your future.

A statement from the telephone company will show you the balance brought forward from last month, any payments that you have paid in the interim and the amount of services that you have consumed this current month, etc., etc. Finally you are told of the new balance that you owe and this is expressed in dollars.

The statement provides you with vital information that you can use and benefit from particularly if you are in the process of planning your finances for the present or future times.

However, the type of financial plan that we usually visualise is a document that focuses specifically on the future, providing sufficient appropriate financial data so that you can form an idea in terms of cost or income, enabling you to make informed decisions. Yes, this is generally what we think about when we talk of a financial plan.

Financial plans should never be thought of in casual terms because finance related matters can constitute an important part of everyone's life in almost every aspect.

Many people can be easily confused when reading financial plans, sometimes due to the content or perhaps the manner in which the plan is set out. This is particularly so in books written by so-called financial experts.

It would seem that the author of such a volume assumes that the reader fully understands money matters to the extent that they do themselves, and consequently they fail to give sufficient thought to the interpretation that is needed to unravel the confusion that the lay reader sees in front of them.

Not so here I trust. Being an ordinary person with average intelligence, my accounting knowledge is derived mainly as a part of my professional work experience and so I hope that everything in this book in viewed in basic, everyday language, especially the parts that refer to matters of finance.

I'm sure you will agree that it is very important that you fully understand my style of presentation so that you can adapt the information for your own particular use. How else will you plot your retirement income that is meant to provide you with those golden years?

IMPORTANT POINT

**DON'T BE IN A RUSH TO
TOSS OUT UNWANTED MAIL**

TAKE YOUR TIME

**MISTAKES CAN OFTEN BE MADE
WHEN THINGS ARE DONE IN A HURRY!**

FOUR STAGES FOR YOUR INCOMING MAIL

Let's take a closer look at some of those financial documents we just referred to. For example, what do you usually do with any unsolicited mail that comes to your home? Any financial paper or letter that you receive, no matter what the level of importance should be treated in at least four fundamental stages even unconsciously, because at this point, you will not know the content or the information. Its implications could possibly have a major affect on your future.

Therefore, and I know this is very basic but never-the-less here it is. The various stages that you might take when receiving a letter could be as follows:

You read it.

You understand it, or if not, you ask questions.

You digest it. You give the matter some thought for a moment allowing the ramifications to sink in.

You respond to it. Either trash it or prepare a reply.

IMPORTANT POINT

PERSONAL IDENTITY FRAUD!

ALWAYS SHRED DOCUMENTS THAT CONTAIN PERSONAL INFORMATION SUCH AS NAME, ADDRESS AND DATE OF BIRTH

NEVER SHARE YOUR SOCIAL INSURANCE NUMBER WITH ANYBODY

You read it. Every month we receive letters of some sort in the mail that contain documents about finance, most of them totally unsolicited. They may be in the form of an offer of a credit card, a bank statement or perhaps a letter from the bank about your account. But whatever it is you should never underestimate the important information that it may contain and you are urged to make the necessary time to sit down and read the document in detail until you understand its content. The letter that you discard and trash (and we all are guilty of doing this from time to time) may be the introduction of a lower insurance rate for your car that you could use or it may be from your mortgage company with details of a new style of mortgage that could save you thousands of pounds. But until you read the document thoroughly and understand the content you will never know what the value of the document could mean to you and your pocketbook.

You understand it. We all tend to be so busy in our working life that whenever we receive mail, there is a temptation to discard anything that we do not immediately understand assuming it to be unnecessary in our life and that we can do very well without it. Of course, sometimes this is true, but it only requires one major error and the cost to you could be many hundreds of dollars. So you need to train yourself to appreciate the real potential of all letters that arrive in the mailbox and recognise that to casually discard the wrong one could deny you the opportunity of saving yourself small fortunes. You need to clearly understand what message is being said in the correspondence and while perhaps remaining sceptical, continue to ask questions about the content until you really understand what it is all about. Only then will you be in a position to make a judgement as to whether or not the offer is of any use to you.

You digest it. Now that you understand the content and fully appreciate what is being offered you are in a good position to consider it carefully, perhaps over a cup of coffee while sitting in a comfortable chair. You need to take your time to digest the meaning of the details and how they can affect your future life. You may want to put it through the SWOT analysis test. This is a simple test whereby you analyse a situation from four perspectives.

> Strengths
> Weaknesses
> Opportunities
> Threats

Sometimes this simple procedure can provide you with the platform on which to give more careful consideration to a particular issue and may even bring out the potential that otherwise could remain concealed.

You consider the strengths of the argument or the proposal on offer. You then look at the other side of the coin and consider the counter-arguments or perhaps any disadvantages of the offer. Then you look at the opportunities that the argument opens up for you. The offer itself may mean little to you and have small value but perhaps it has potential and therefore offers an opportunity for something big in the future. Finally you consider the threats. While there may be advantages for you to accept the offer, there may be undisclosed ramifications that if accepted or implemented would be activated and work against you. So consider all of the options and then you will be better able to make a judgement call.

You respond to it. Having taken the first three steps and by doing so, avoided the mistake of discarding the financial document as some useless marketing pamphlet, you are now in the strong position to respond to whatever it is on offer. At least now, if you bin the letter, it will be an informed decision and you will rest easily by knowing that nothing of value has escaped your attention.

Personal Identity Fraud Alert!

One final point. If your name and address is on the letter you will do well to either tear the first page into little pieces or to shred it. Should your date of birth be included, this is especially dangerous and very useful to fraudsters. This combined personal information should never be thrown away in one piece. Major fraud practices include Personal Identity Theft and these three pieces of personal i.d. are highly prized by fraudsters everywhere.

Smoke and mirror time

Financial Plans can be particularly confusing by the manner in which they are presented. You may have heard of this type of practice *as Smoke and Mirrors.* For example, the sender of an unbelievable offer may only wish to disclose to you, (the prospective purchaser) one side of the story, in which case financial figures can be presented highlighting the up-side or a financial surplus with little or no information on any disadvantages.

There may also be a financial loss involved in the offer but the writer has elected to omit this information and so only one side of the story is explained. This practice could also be called trickery.

It is at these times when the experienced financially astute person will hear alarm bells ringing and jot down some questions that need to be asked.

SMOKE AND MIRROR EXAMPLE

I recall a recent incident where a local automobile dealer was advertising *"0% Financing Available for All New Cars!!!"* The smart buyers were asking to see the small print before they signed and only then did they discover that while it was "0% Financing", it was in fact ZERO POINT NINE PERCENT (0.9%) financing. The point nine percent (.9%) had been conveniently omitted from the ad. The difference on a car costing $25,000 could be about $225 for each year of the bank loan needed to finance the car. Over a five-year loan period the extra hidden cost to the buyer might be around ONE THOUSAND DOLLARS. If you were in full time employment and paying income tax you would need to earn over $1,200.00 to be left with the cost of this quite significant hidden amount of money.

Of course, the charge would be included on the bill of sale and included in the small print, but you likely wouldn't see it as it would possibly be included in with the extras such as delivery, licensing, upgrades, special wheels, air conditioning tax, sales tax and all those other costs that are added to the basic price of a car.

This practice is fraudulent, dishonest and devious but never the less it happens to the unwary purchaser. You should be certain that it doesn't happen to you.

Remember, always be sure to read the small print so as to see through the clouds of smoke and mirrors and never sign anything in a hurry. As Polly used always to say to me, "So long as you have your money still in your pocket you are in the driving seat and so retain the strength when negotiating." There will always be another car, or fridge or house that you will fall in love with and so, take your time to consider what is on offer and if necessary, sleep on it. It will still be there in the morning." Good advice indeed.

Similarly, auto insurance companies will charge you about an extra fifty dollars each year to provide you with a protection for your 5* Rating. In essence, this means that if you have an accident and it is your fault your good driving record will be protected and you will not be penalized for having one accident in any given year. However, when the insurance year expires and the time comes for you to shop around, to your amazement you discover that frequently, the practice used is that the protection is only good if you stay with your current insurance company. To shift to a different insurance company will deny you the opportunity to benefit from your former excellent driving record.

I am told that this accident can stay on your driving record for as long as five or even seven years. Furthermore, my insurers recently disclosed to me that if I do not ask or remind them of the protection arrangement at the time of the policy renewal each year, they will overlook it and I will not receive it! More smoke and mirrors?

IMPORTANT POINT

**DO NOT BE HURRIED TO
SIGN ON THE DOTTED LINE**

ALWAYS READ THE SMALL PRINT

INHERITING A WINDFALL

Have you ever pondered what you would do if you won the lottery or otherwise came into a fortune? Probably. Because most people will have some sort of a windfall at some point in their lives and it can come in many forms.

It could be a lottery win (which is what we all hope for) but more likely to be an award in some other form such as a legacy or a share distribution due to a company takeover with whom you own stock. It could even be something less sophisticated such as a Las Vegas style jackpot payout on a fruit machine.

What would you do with such a welcome surprise? How would you go about deciding where to spend it and how much to spend? Of course, the immediate reaction is to celebrate somehow perhaps with close friends and family, but that can be dangerous too. Most people are only jealous in such a circumstance and family members can be even worse.

We are told that a meal-out or an exotic vacation are the commonest forms of celebrating a win and that is o.k. if the cost is moderate. But what if it is a significant windfall, maybe as much as several hundred thousand dollars, then what?

Spending is fun and if your spending spree is done in moderation then fine but be sure that your splash will not be the cause for regret later in life if you fall on hard times!

And so, what would I do if I inherited say, $1,000,000?

Well, remember that at my age, I do not have too many future years to worry about and I also have some solid savings behind me as well as regular pensions that provide very well for the usual needs for Polly and me each month. But if say, I was in my forties or fifties, I suppose this is how I would share the booty.

I would pay off any mortgage that I might have.

I would set aside $200,000 for immediate use. Fun things like celebrations and gifts to family members as well as paying off their mortgages. That may help them to get a good start in life.

I would set aside the balance for a rainy day – invest it at minimal risk with two or three banks. That would give me a return of about three or four per-cent. If the capital amount to invest was say, $600,000, at 4% the yearly interest would amount to $24,000. Of course, this amount would be added to my annual income for income tax purposes and after that, the yield may reduce to about $17,000. But remember, the capital and the interest will remain in the account and so the second year I will have a balance of around $617,010 on which to earn another 4%. Again, the power of compounding would reveal itself. I would earn interest on the interest.

All interest earned from the bank or anywhere else is subject to income tax of course, but this would be a nice money tree to forget about. It would be there for as long as we wanted so that Polly or I would have the protection that it would afford us for our twilight years.

What are your current financial plans?

But back to the topic of Financial Plans, and the question here is, "Do you currently have any financial plans?"

If you have a budget then the answer is yes. If you have a written plan for a vacation and it includes any financially related material then again, yes, you do have a financial plan. You may have a list of payments that you make each month that come directly out of your bank account. If this is the case, then that is another financial plan.

WHAT ARE YOUR DEBTS?

What about your DEBTS? Most of us have these. Do you know what these are and how much the total amount is that you owe?

Do you have a plan to pay off your debts? If you have answered "NO!" then my response is that you should have a plan.

You need to know how much your debt is costing you each year. The answer may propel you to pay off the debt sooner. Remember what we talked about earlier in the book. It is better to RECEIVE interest than to PAY interest. Well, the sooner you can get on to that track, the sooner you will become wealthy and financially independent.

Many people find it necessary to visit their local community office to obtain help so as to sort out their major debt problem. Do this if you need to and do it soon. Major debt is a great worry to many people and can creep up on you from nowhere and take over your life like an addiction. Seek help as soon as possible. If you can sort out the mess yourself with the help of your bank then better still. You will feel that you are in charge and that you are taking control, which, I am told is a good feeling to have in such a circumstance. Here is one way you can go about it.

Identify the total debt that you have by writing down the amount of any payments that you need to make each month.

Identify all of your net monthly income. Write down the total amount that is credited to your bank account each month.

Split your everyday living costs into 2 sections –
a.fixed costs
b.variable costs

Fixed Costs.

Fixed costs are the regular payments that you need to find money for each month. They are usually the same amount each month and they are the expenses that you have little or no choice over. These fixed costs might include:

Rent or Mortgage

Not much choice here. You need shelter whatever your situation. However, if you need to make savings, perhaps you can reduce the cost by downsizing or moving into a less expensive neighbourhood.

FOOD

Preparing your own meals is the most cost-efficient way of eating. Buy your food at the cheaper supermarkets. You know the ones I mean. The food is fresh and the prices are less. Use a box or take bags with you. Remember, every nickel or dime you spend unnecessarily, is money wasted. This carefree approach to budgeting and spending has to stop.

Focus on the fact that you have a major debt and that you will need to change your spending habits BIG TIME. Buying pre-prepared food is costly and these packaged items usually contain preservatives.

Salads and fresh vegetables are nutritious and can be obtained cheaply. Look for the cheaper cuts of meat and fish. Spend more time cooking at the stove and less time in the coffee shops. I am speaking to the male readers here too – in fact especially to the male readers. If you need to make major savings then cut out or cut down on the coffees, lunches, prepared sandwiches and soup counters. A cup of soup from a package usually only needs hot water and is warming and very cost efficient. Soup drank with Pita bread can make a nourishing lunchtime meal. Try eating smaller portions. Take a look at yourself. If you are overweight then maybe that is where all your money has gone!

ELECTRICITY, GAS AND WATER

These fixed costs are necessary for you to survive. But turning out lights when not being used can result in major savings. Also, I am told that if you unplug the TV when not in use, this can result in significant annual savings. Remember how the TV would take minutes to warm up before it produced a picture? Well, seemingly the manufacturers responded to the consumer demand to have instant TV and so that convenience comes with a cost. It appears that the TV is really on all the time so that it is warmed up and ready for us to use instantly when we want it.

Gas or oil savings may be possible too by turning the heat down a notch or two. Instead of having a five-minute shower, try a two-minute one. Any savings on hot water will result in savings from the heating bill. Shorter time under the shower will also save on the amount of water that you use which in turn, results in cost savings on your water bill.

CAR PAYMENT

There is not much savings to be made here unless you want the car to be re-possessed by the bank or the lease company. However, review your options and consider if you really need the car that you have. Perhaps you could settle for a less expensive car or one that would burn less gas. A small car may attract a cheaper insurance rate too and so there could be a double savings for you.

Consider whether it is really necessary for you to have a car? Many people get around very well using public transport and while it may not be as convenient, just think of your investment sitting outside the workplace all day, continually rotting and eroding and depreciating in value while you are inside, working hard every day to pay for it.

Variable costs

Variable costs are the selective costs and expenses that you incur each month. With many of these you have a choice. There are exceptions to this category such as medical, dental and prescription glasses. While they may not be regular fixed costs, they represent expenses that you likely cannot avoid. Other variable costs could be restaurant charges, gasoline costs for going off on impulsive trips somewhere, movies, lottery tickets, sports events, personal leisure activities, spectator events, exhibitions, shows, clothes, shoes, and the list goes on.

I am not saying that you should not participate in leisure past times or making purchases that you want rather than what you need, but if you are serious about reducing your debt then you really need to adjust your thinking so as to re-balance your spending habits. The stores are full of attractive things and the packaging makes everything look so appealing. But it is designed that way and you need to exercise some self-constraint if you expect to have a sizeable nest egg when you are in your sixties.

So just think about what you are doing and what you are spending and more importantly, how you are spending your money and what exactly you are getting for it. Watch out for those smoke and mirrors!

When you have written down that list of your income and your expenses, scrutinise the expenses and see if there are any items that you can eliminate from the monthly cost. Cell phones are fun and convenient. You probably have a cell phone for an emergency. If you have a major debt, you cannot afford a cell phone. When considering what you can cut down on, be ruthless. You need to be. You are in serious trouble and you need to take serious action, NOW!

Next, take a good look at your income. If you have serious debt then maybe you are not earning enough. You need to earn more money. You need to work more hours. You probably do not work on weekends and so you have time to wander around the stores being tempted to spend money that you don't have.

Get a part time weekend job. This will not only keep you out of the stores, it will also provide you with some extra money – maybe even as much as $100.00 each week. After a year you will have $5,200! After 5-years you will have an extra $26,000!

I know that this all seems very cold and hard but these are hard times. You can do it. You just need to get started.

Concentrate on chipping away at the problem in little bits. That way it will seem achievable. Mountains are hard to climb but lots of little hills can be managed with a small amount of effort. You can do it! Good Luck.

SMOKE AND MIRRORS - A final word

A final word about Smoke and Mirrors. The "*smoke and mirror*" part of this Chapter comes from a very old expression which is thought to have emanated from the theatre. Experienced conjurers or magicians would use smoke or mirrors to deceive the audience as part of their act. Some artists would often use both smoke *and* mirrors and so this reference was used when referring to business deals or the like.

A deal would be presented to an unsuspecting customer as a genuine opportunity with a potential financial gain. In truth, it was shady and cooked up by using bogus numbers. This would bolster the gain-factor and thus present the appearance that the benefit to the customer would be significantly more valuable than it actually was. "*Smoke and Mirrors.*" You might say that this is a nicely put expression for trickery.

IMPORTANT POINT

WILL YOUR PENSION NEED MAGIC TO

MAKE IT A REALITY?

It is important to watch out for smoke and mirrors when you are presented with any opportunity. It might be in a furniture store, on a used-car lot or at a time-share purchase seminar. Even financial institutions have been known to misrepresent figures in an effort to zealously encourage customers to invest or to buy in a particular venture.

And so, beware! When you are presented with any financial plan. While it may *appear* to be exactly as it is being presented, it is of vital importance for you to KNOW that it is exactly that - a genuine representation of what you believe it to be.

Never permit yourself to be mesmerised by those magicians and conjurors by their *smoke and mirrors.* Deception is not for you.

Chapter six
INVESTMENT ADVISER
How can I pick a good one?

An experienced investment adviser or fund manager is an essential ingredient of your retirement plan. If you employ a good one, their skill, together with their great knowledge of the financial markets can help your savings grow more than you would probably have believed possible. But be careful. As with everything in life, fund managers come in all shapes and sizes and are packaged in a variety of ways.

Many people have been persuaded to hand over the trust of their funds to well educated and fast talking fund managers, only to discover at a later stage that their funds were used for other purposes and all but disappeared. This happens in many countries in the world and fortunately such cases are rare. However, just the same, it is important that you should know at the beginning of this chapter exactly what is out there and who is out there so that there can be no surprises.

Personally, I have always had a problem finding a good fund manager, particularly when I was starting on my retirement plan. At that time, outstanding professional fund managers were few and far between. They were rare individuals indeed and so to find a good one was rather like looking for the proverbial needle in a haystack. There was no benchmark by which to make a judgment call.

Most people had accountants to do their taxes and look after their money-related issues in those days and Polly and I were no different. Not that our finances were difficult, but we had a good friend who was an accountant and so it was convenient and easier to get Stephen to work out our tax returns for us.

He would also suggest where we should put any savings and would set up our R. R. S. P. (Registered Retirement Savings Plan) funds. At that time, many people put their savings in Guaranteed Investment Certificates (G.I.C.'s) or Canada Savings Bonds (C.S.B.'s) until mutual funds became more fashionable.

One of the attractions of mutual funds for the ordinary person was that they would respond to the stock market fluctuations while not committing you to actually buy any shares directly. Also, as it was quickly pointed out to us, it was prudent to invest in a mix of funds. Mutual, cash and bonds. That way, if the stock markets went down, the cash associated investments or the bond type of investments would, under most conditions, remain steady. You could also buy a mutual fund that itself was diversified as most of them are now.

Investing in that manner provided your portfolio with some protection. You reduced the risk of finding that your entire savings had evaporated overnight.

And so, every year in late March or early April, Polly and I would make the annual trek to Stephen's office armed with a couple of large envelopes that contained our financial records for the preceding twelve-month period.

Gradually as the years went by, from time to time at dinner parties or other social gatherings when conversations got around to finances, we would hear people talk of financial planners and fund managers. This was something new to Polly and me as it was to most people. We had always felt comfortable with Stephen and so we never felt the need for a professional manager to look after our savings. In any event, as we probably had less than about six-month's salary saved, there was hardly a need for a professional manager. We merely bought G.I.C.'s or C.S.B.'s as our R.R.S.P. contribution and forgot about them until it was tax time again. In those days the interest rates were around 14 or 15 per cent!

I also remember wondering about the *cost* of hiring a fund manager and what would I get in reply for the fees. Nobody works for nothing and one could safely assume that a fund manager was a professionally qualified person, perhaps with a university degree and so of course, they would expect to earn a substantial income for managing hundreds of thousands of dollars of clients' savings. After all, that would be a huge responsibility and so high fees for such a person would be likely. The more that I thought about it the more I was put off from doing anything. "Just another cost that I can do without." I thought to myself.

Some years later, a job opportunity came to my attention that would take me to Europe for what appeared to be a period of time exceeding possibly ten years. The Employer Pension Plan that was with the company I worked for was separate from any GIC's or other savings that we had accumulated. We needed to make a decision.

Should we leave the Employer Pension Plan it where it was and allow it to grow steadily within the collective plan or should we remove it and transfer it to a large financial organisation that specialised in managing investment portfolios for people like us.

This was to be a major decision and one that we shouldn't take lightly, after all, there was a lot at stake and much to be considered.

What were the pros and the cons? At times like this, I would always take a large sheet of paper and draw a line down the middle. On the left side of the line I would write a list of numbers one through ten. I would do likewise on the right side of the paper. Next, on the left side of the sheet of paper, beside each of the numbers, I would write down the advantages of taking action, in this case, to transfer my savings out from the pension group that they were currently with. On the right side of the sheet of paper I would write down beside each of the numbers a list of the disadvantages of taking action.

The benefit of taking this simple step is to be able to immediately view how many advantages and how many disadvantages there are. Also, the process directs your full attention to the problem and forces you to expand your thinking processes. In doing so, you frequently discover that there are many more things to write down than you first realized.

Among the advantages that we could think of were as follows: As we were going to be out of Canada, we may not be aware of any major happenings that could influence our portfolio either way. To remove our pension savings to a fund manager might provide us with a margin of safety that we might otherwise not have.

As our retirement years were still thought to be about ten or fifteen years away, we could afford to take a higher level of risk with our portfolio. This in turn would provide an opportunity for more growth. A fund under the management of a major financial investment company could have the benefit to select more aggressive mutual funds that would address that preference.

The current portfolio was lodged in a single pension fund with a large institution. While it was considered quite safe and perhaps the individual investments within the fund were diversified, the total savings in the fund itself were not.

If the operation of the institution itself ceased, what would happen to the pension fund?

If the pension fund went to the wall, so would our total pension portfolio.

With the new arrangement we would have more flexibility and would have the option to change our minds on the types of investments if we wanted. We could make adjustments according to the prevailing global economic conditions.

The list of disadvantages that transferring our portfolio would create included some of the above as well as some of the following:

If we transferred the pension fund we would be giving a significant amount of our savings to an untried firm to manage and sometimes they might need to make decisions on our behalf.

We would be living about four thousand miles away with time zone differentials. How accessible would the new fund managers be if we needed to speak to them about an issue?

What would the cost be? We had heard that professional fund managers could charge high fees. We had also heard of commissions and trailing commissions. What exactly were these costs? Were they totally transparent? How much would we be paying for this new service?

What if the new fund managers invested our pension savings in a very aggressive fund and we lost everything?

There might have been some additional concerns for either side but as I recall it, these were the main issues. What would you have done?

We struggled with the dilemma for quite some time, but a decision had to be made. At the same time, I had to get myself installed into my new position and learn the ropes of the new job. While I was doing this, Polly stayed in Canada and sold our home and made the necessary arrangements to ship our furniture and personal effects to Europe.

Eventually, we made a decision. It was to transfer the pension funds and go with the fund manager. In my absence, Polly signed the legal documents that she was permitted to and any that required my signature she sent to me by overnight courier.

We have always been pleased with that decision, or at least the decision to remove the savings from the pension fund and invest it into mutual funds. It grew more than we ever expected. To be fair though, the main cause of this was the major growth that the global markets were experiencing. The fund manager was partly responsible for the growth but not totally.

During the eleven years that we were out of Canada we stayed totally loyal to my retirement plan. It would have been easy to cash-in some of our unlocked savings plans that we had in Canada, converted the dollars to local currency and lived the good life, but that was not a part of the plan when I prepared it.

It was very tempting I can tell you. Very tempting. Especially when Polly wanted to buy a larger house than our budget would permit or when I wanted to buy a larger car than we could afford. But no, we bit the bullet, left the money in Canada and that was one of the best decisions that we ever made.

We made a conscious decision to let our lifestyle be controlled by the amount of local income that we could generate while we were abroad. What we could not afford we would go without!

It was a terrible struggle at first for a variety of reasons. Our furniture was too large for those smaller houses and so we needed to replace nearly all of our furniture. Also, the electrical system was different and so all of our electrically powered appliances would need to be replaced with local ones. The spending went on and on, without using any of our Canadian savings. We were hurting but at the same time, we were being smart. We were sticking to our game plan within the confines of our overall Retirement Plan and that was the main thing at that time.

We thought and hoped that we would reap the benefits later and now of course we are, although, while we were away, we were constantly on the lookout for an investment opportunity that would add something to our nest egg. I suppose we had always done that.

I remember many years ago, before we left Canada, my good friend Roy called me and asked me if Polly and I would be interested in going away with Joan and him on a weekend jaunt to Lagoon City.

"Where on earth is that?" I asked.

"Oh, not far." replied Roy. "It's about an hour's drive from Toronto, up Highway 48, near Lake Simcoe". "They're offering a special weekend." "It's an investment opportunity. They want to sell land with harbour access and some chalets, so they are offering a weekend away for twenty-five bucks".

"It includes Saturday afternoon and evening with dinner and a dance; a breakfast on the Sunday morning with a buffet lunch before departure." "Not bad eh?" Roy sounded really upbeat about it. He always liked a bargain.

The line went dead. "Are you still there Robert?" Roy inquired.

"Yes Roy, I'm still here."

"Well, what do you think?"

"Sounds good to me Roy." "Is that twenty-five dollars each?"

"No, you idiot!" His Irish accent coming to the fore. "Would I spend fifty-bucks just to listen to a sales pitch?" "It's twenty-five dollars a couple, and each couple gets a chalet to themselves with a log-burning fireplace. And the meals are included".

"Sounds terrific Roy." "I'll definitely speak to Polly when she comes in and we'll call you back."

We did call them back and we did all go to Lagoon City for the weekend.

It was fun and we were very impressed with what we were shown in the area. Of course, at that time there was nothing much finished. Nothing there to speak of, but they were selling from the plans and Roy and Joan were always on the lookout for a good investment opportunity, as were we. And of course, a cheap weekend away was good too!.

Polly has always been afraid of being near water. It can generate her panic attacks but on the Sunday morning, we found Roy and Joan relaxing in the hot tub. Polly sat on the side as I jumped in and joined them. We talked about the place and how impressed we were with the plans that we had seen.

"Is this the sort of place that you would like to invest in Robert?" Joan asked.

"To be honest Joan," I answered, "about three weeks ago I was introduced to an investment adviser and so while I haven't signed up with them yet, I think that it might be a good idea if I consult with them first."

"Oh really?" queried Joan seeming somewhat surprised. Investment advisers were a rare breed in those days. "An investment adviser. Mmm. Who is he?"

"It isn't a he, it's a HER," I responded as the steam rose from the hot tub into the cooler air.

"Ah ah! Do you know about this Polly?" We all laughed aloud.

"Of course I do Joan." Polly replied. "It was me who introduced Robert to her."

"So what's the attraction of having an investment adviser Robert?"

I explained that I was getting increasingly busy at work, and while I may not exactly need one at the moment, I would like to check into it just to be informed. I was finding it increasingly difficult to find the amount of time necessary to maintain proper control on any savings we had. Also, with more and more funds coming onto the market, I was unsure as to where precisely to place my savings. And so, if we could find a professional investment counsellor who could advise us, we would be interested in handing things over so to speak.

Depending on the cost of course, and this is where it really gets interesting.

Have you ever tried to knit with spaghetti? Well I haven't either, but if you have ever attempted to establish the fees that are charged by an investment counsellor then you have a pretty good idea.

To simplify the understanding of fees charged by investment managers could be very straightforward. A simplified process would make clients feel more comfortable due to the fact that they would know exactly how much they were paying for the service provided by their hired professional. After all, that is precisely what they are. A Hired Professional. Just like a lawyer or an accountant.

Would you hire an accountant without knowing the cost? You can be sure that you will know the cost sooner or later as they will no doubt provide you with an invoice. And if you need to use a lawyer (another hired professional), then again, you may rest assured that you will receive an invoice at some stage in your business dealings.

The number of different fund managers that I have used during my life has been about six. I have never once received an invoice, a statement of account or any other document that provides me with a detailed account of the costs. The best that I have heard is from my current hired professional who advises me that their fees are up to one-point-five percent of the total funds invested. No more. They earn other money from commissions and trailing commissions.

Now in fact, this is quite a good rate and not as bad as it seems. I will tell you why.

Some fund managers charge fees for each fund they manage and the amount of the fee charged is based on the value of the particular fund that they manage. There may be other incentives, some hidden, that work against you but more about that later.

IMPORTANT POINT

WHEN HIRING A FUND MANAGER

**REQUEST A WRITTEN EXPLANATION
OF ALL CHARGES THAT WILL
BE MADE TO YOUR FUND ACCOUNTS**

The up side of this particular arrangement is this. If the manager's income is commensurate with the value of your fund; isn't there an incentive for the manager to *increase* the value of your fund.? Right! But it isn't always like this.

All fund managers should always have an incentive to increase the value of your funds. This is in your interest and after all, you are the customer.

If a particular fund manager or investment counsellor is not prepared to clearly identify their charges, then one can only assume that they have something to hide. But perhaps don't blame the manager. If it is corporate policy then they are only following the company protocol.

Over the years I have been so frustrated with this sort of smoke and mirrors activity that I have been left with no option but to move on.

To be fair, in the early days the blame was probably mine for not standing toe-to-toe with the manager and insisting on receiving a detailed list of the fees that I would be expected to pay. I suppose as a younger person I was intimidated as I was unsure of the rules. I also hadn't got very much money. But there will be no excuses for you now that you know the rules. Ask the questions and do not be intimidated.

HIDDEN INCENTIVE

Earlier, I made comment about an incentive for financial managers. To perhaps more fully understand where we are going with this, it might be helpful to know exactly what an incentive is. The dictionary that I am currently using describes the word as follows:

Quote: **Incentive** *a motivating influence; stimulus. An additional payment made to employees as a means of increasing production. Etc., etc.* End of Quote.

Increasing production? I think that I would have felt happier if the explanation had been something like this; "*An additional payment made to employees as a means of increasing the value of service to a customer or client*". But that was not the case and neither is it. Therefore,, I am left to deduce that any incentive that is awarded to a manager is one that will work against the customer, that is you and me.

The incentive that you and I should know about is the *reward* that is paid to the fund manager on occasion when a particular fund is sold or bought. We might perhaps be more familiar with the term commission. But this is rarely spelled out to us in the spoken word or the large print that is within a contract document. It can be seen however in small print in circumstances where a commission or a trailing commission is paid to the fund manager.

"But wait a minute," I hear you calling to me. "If my fund manager has an opportunity to receive a commission or an incentive to sell my funds or to buy me new funds, doesn't he or she have a conflict of interest?"

Congratulations! You have just identified a very important point. You may just want to climb up to the cupboard and get down that old box of investment papers and scrutinise the small print.

Take a good look and jot down the frequency of the purchase of new funds and the dates of the sale of your other funds. Indeed, you may feel that it is time to pick up the phone and make an appointment to sit down with your fund manager and have a heart-to heart. Remember, you are the client. You are the customer and you are paying to your manager an agreed fee to have your funds managed in a professional fashion.

If incentives are payable to your manager, then of course, all might be well, but you may also take the position that you should have been notified of the details. Furthermore, why isn't the fund manager's employer paying out the incentive?

You may remember when you started to read this book, many pages ago the question was asked, "Where am I now?" I uttered on about how important it was that you should know exactly the value of your savings. What you have and where it was.

Now perhaps you are beginning to see the wisdom in knowing everything about your funds. Current information is important and only possible by maintaining an up to date chart of your funds. This way, you can refer to what you have, when you bought it, how much you paid for it and if it is quoted on the stock market, what the symbol is and what the month-end value is.

Remember, the more information you have at hand the easier it will be to track your Retirement Plan.

So now you know something about a good fund manager. They should have honesty, integrity, experience, loyalty and knowledge. But there is more.

An outstanding fund manager should also be *available*. Let me relate to you an experience that occurred to me when we were on our second fund manager. By the way, we left our first fund manager due to the fact that whenever we met with the individual, which usually was once a year, almost all of our questions remained unanswered. In addition, the growth that we saw happening in the global markets just didn't happen in our particular funds.

Our second fund manager came about partly as a result of wanting to change institutions and so we carefully investigated the services on offer from the banking institution that we used for our main bank accounts. We had been a customer with them for many years and as they were one of Canada's largest, we thought that it was a good place to start.

We made an appointment to see the bank manager and explained our situation.

"Mr. & Mrs. Kite, we would be delighted to have your business," we were assured. "In fact, we have a special scheme in place so that the transition from the other institution should be a worry-free activity for you both."

"Oh, that's good to hear because we were concerned as to how we would go about moving our portfolio from one large firm to another," Polly responded.

"Most people are." we were told, "Now, If you will excuse me for a moment I will just go and see if Mr. Greene is available. He is our senior fund manager and you will like him I feel sure".

"Thank you Mr. Chong," I replied.

As he walked out of the office and along the carpeted hallway, Polly looked at me with one eyebrow raised.

"What do you think," she asked.

"I'm not sure," I replied. "But I'll have a better idea this time next year."

"Your so clever Darling'" she said sarcastically, adding, "That's why I love you so much". We laughed. After a few minutes, Mr. Chong returned.

"Here we are," he said as he arrived at the office door. "Bob, I would like you to meet Mr. & Mrs. Kite."

"How do you do," said Mr Greene as he offered his hand.

After the introductions we followed Bob Greene to his office. It seemed very well fitted out and I wondered if our fees were going to be paying for all of this seemingly unnecessary luxury. Anyway, we sat down and we were provided with a presentation that included the services that we would receive and how we would benefit from moving our business to Mr. Greene.

We were careful to ask about charges and while we listened to the answers, I am not sure if we really understood the detail of what we were being told. I remember the word MER being mentioned and I remember that this was something new to me.

"What exactly is MER?" I asked.

"MER is an acronym for Management Expense Ratio," he replied. "It represents the total fees charged for management expenses and operating expenses and it is expressed as a percentage of the fund's average daily assets".

"Will there be any other costs or fees or will that be the total of what we will be paying for your services, Mr. Greene?" I asked.

"Well, yes, there will no doubt be a few more costs that you should know about," he replied.

I got the distinct impression that Bob felt a bit uncomfortable that I was delving into the charges in such detail. Also, I am not too sure if we would have received an explanation had I not pressed him.

He then went on to explain that MER did not include commissions or taxes.

I learned that the cost of the MER would be charged to our savings fund. I was assured that this was normal.

In other words, while your savings may grow, the amount of the growth will be decreased by all of the charges that will be made to your fund.

MER represents just one of those charges. In addition there may be taxes and commissions to pay. Again these costs will be paid by you and will likely be taken directly out of your fund. The effect is that your fund will decrease in value from its original earnings.

Things to remember:

It is usual for the returns on funds to be quoted with the MER costs already deducted.

A prospectus for a mutual fund will always disclose the MER that will be charged for the respective fund.

In Canada, the MER rate can vary and the range is generally from 0.5% to 3%. Possibly more that this on funds with foreign content as there can be increased research work required on the part of the fund managers. This cost has to be met.

If your investments happen to be *actively* managed then the MER rate will usually be higher.

While the details of these charges are made available to all customers, for some reason they seem to maintain a low profile, such as being typed in very small print or provided on the reverse side of a document that you would need to sign.

"Mr. Greene. Are mutual funds guaranteed or insured?" Polly asked.

"No, Mrs. Kite, they are not." Mr Greene replied. "Some types of investments are, such as G.I.C.'s, but with mutual funds the investment is not guaranteed and the investment is not insured."

"I suppose that is why when we hear TV commercials for funds we are told that mutual funds can go down as well as up and that past performance is no guarantee of future growth", Polly commented.

"That's right." Mr. Greene replied. "It is a legal requirement that all prospective purchasers are forewarned of what could happen even though the likelihood of it happening can be somewhat remote."

Other information we obtained included:

No-Load funds. These do not have a sales charge.

Front-End or Back-End Loaded Funds. These DO have a sales charge.

Some of the main advantages of Mutual Funds are:

Ability to hold a diversification or a mixed bag of funds

Funds are usually handled by professional managers

Availability of a variety of purchase plans

Availability of a variety of types of plans

Quite liquid and transferable

Quite convenient

Some of the disadvantages are:

> Unknown ability of the fund manager
> Difficulty in identifying the exact costs
> Vulnerability, common within the marketplace

After our questions had been dealt with we thanked Mr. Greene for his time and said that we would discuss the information and get back to him in a few days. In fact, we did - and made an appointment to attend his office to sign the relevant documentation.

A week or two later, we entered the bank and met with Bob Greene. There seemed to be many sheets of paper to sign but it all seemed to go smoothly. We were assured that we would receive a confirmation in the mail. Also, that each month we would receive a statement for each of the portfolios showing the details of the funds that we held and their current values.

Bob seemed a pleasant guy. He was a family man and explained to us that he lived a little way out of the city but he enjoyed the drive in, enjoying the beautiful Ontario scenery as he did so.

He told us that he and his wife enjoyed the cottage country and that they had a waterfront property. "It's like going away on vacation every evening when I drive home from a day's work," Bob told us.

After about an hour, Polly and I found ourselves walking out of the bank, pleased with our decision and looking forward to the change in our investment management.

"Happy?" I asked her, squeezing her hand as we walked the short distance to the car.

"Are you, Robert?" Polly returned the question.

"I think so, Polly." The atmosphere was quiet as we drove away to do some shopping. Both of us were engrossed in our personal thoughts.

I remember thinking at the time what a giant step it was to change our investment adviser. After all, they were in charge of our life savings for the most part, and their decisions could cost us dearly if they were the wrong ones.

Of course, they could also make us a lot of money if their decisions were the right ones. "Oh well," I said to Polly. "We'll find out in due course."

After a few weeks the large envelopes started to arrive. These were the statements that Bob had told us about. I opened them earnestly, eager to learn what changes he had made. Polly usually left this sort of thing to me and was happy to discuss such matters over dinner. There were five separate funds established, two for Polly, two for me and one in both our names. That arrangement was quite satisfactory, after all, the total savings in reality belonged to both of us and we had agreed with the bank that they should group the funds so that we both would benefit from any tax advantage.

Before long, I was back at the computer, working on my retirement plan adjusting the fund-column entries so as to reflect the changes in the set-up of the investment funds.

Each month, I would look forward to receiving the statements so that I could compare the actual month-end values with spreadsheet details that I had predicted. There were some months when I would be over the moon with excitement and joy as the numbers flowed through the spreadsheet. My retirement plan was telling me that the future was looking very good indeed. But there were also the times when the economy was taking a bashing, the stock markets across Canada and the U.S. were plunging and our future savings looked very sad indeed. Our dinner conversations were very limited during those times. The meal portions seemed to look smaller too.

Six months later, I had a list of questions that I wanted to put to Mr Greene. They had accumulated during the preceding months and rather than disturb him with just a question or two, I thought that it would be best to wait until I had sufficient questions to justify a meeting.

I picked up the 'phone and called him. A voicemail message told me the day's date, and that Mr. Greene was in the office but was unavailable at that moment and would be sure to return the call. It concluded by wishing me a "Great Day."

A few days went by. As I hadn't heard from him I punched the number for his office. His voice mail repeated the previous message, but with a change in the date and again, concluded by wishing me a "Great day."

After a few days, Mr. Greene eventually returned the call and we got to speak. He explained that as he lives quite a distance away he now comes into the office only a few days each week. I was disappointed to hear this, but my thought was brief. I scheduled a meeting and Polly and I set off for the appointment.

Our questions were not of major significance but a few specific issues that I wanted clarified. Bob greeted us both and was very helpful on all counts. However, Polly's amazing intuition picked up on some signals that made her feel somewhat uneasy. She was unable to explain her concern in detail but as she put it, it was just a feeling she had. I too had felt something but certainly not to the same degree as Polly.

Six months later it was time to meet with Bob Greene again, this time for our annual review. We were disappointed that it was left to us to initiate the meeting insomuch that the anniversary date came and went and we heard nothing from the bank. After a few telephone calls, we got to speak with Mr. Greene's assistant who kindly set up the appointment.

At the appointed hour, Polly and I arrived at the shopping mall and entered the bank. There was a special suite of offices where the investment side of the business was transacted. We made our way to the small private reception area.

"Good Afternoon Mrs. Kite. Good Afternoon Mr. Kite, said Debbie as she greeted us. "How nice to see you."

"Thank you Debbie and it is good to see you too." replied Polly. "I believe that we have an appointment with Mr. Greene."

"Certainly. Won't you sit down? I won't be a moment."

Debbie disappeared out of our view as she walked into the reserved area.

She returned a short while later. "Angie will be out to see you shortly." said Debbie.

"Angie?" I inquired.

Debbie then explained that Mr. Greene was away on leave for a few months and Angie was looking after his clients in the interim.

Angie appeared, introduced herself and invited us both into her office. My questions were duly answered and Polly also had some queries. These were answered too.

Mr. Greene never returned to the bank. He seemingly took long term disability and so Angie became our new fund manager. But this was only for a year.

Twelve months later when we again appeared for our anniversary meeting we were introduced to a Mr. Khan who explained that Angie was on maternity leave and that he would now be looking after our funds.

This constant shift from fund manager to fund manger totally unnerved us and so our confidence in the bank diminished week by week. Unless we took the initiative, there was no communication between the fund manager and ourselves.

A few months later we moved all of our bank accounts to another bank and our investment portfolios to another fund management institution. That was a few years ago and so far so good.

The point of the story here is to demonstrate that no matter how good the fund is and the resulting growth of your money tree, if the personal relationship is not there then the client (us in this case) has no feeling of being and so is likely to move on.

"A rolling stone gathers no moss," they say, and they are probably right. So Polly and I remain reluctant to make too many more moves.

Chapter Seven
RETIREMENT OBJECTIVES

How much will I need in Retirement?

You remember that old saying – If you don't know where you are going, then any road will get you there?

It sounds amusing I know but in reality, it has merit because if you don't know where you are going and specifically, the place where you want to be, then your destination could in fact be anywhere. And any road or rather, every road will get you somewhere.

Clearly, whatever it is we are planning we need a definitive chart so that we can clearly see the way forward and make adjustments as necessary, otherwise who knows where we may finish up!

The road map must be well thought out, well considered, clearly defined and fully agreed to by all those people that it affects, the stake holders if you like. The road to retirement is simply that. A road map taking you from your present situation to somewhere you would rather be or in this case, somewhere you are inescapably heading for but of course, when you arrive there, you might like to be in a different situation, financially speaking.

The fact that you are now planning your retirement by assessing your current wealth, estimating how much you can save each month and projecting forward the size that your money tree will have grown to by the time you reach retirement age demonstrates clearly that you have made the adjustment. That you have come to terms with the fact that retirement for you will not be an accident but rather, the result of a plan.

You are in control of an embryonic Retirement Plan and once firmly established, you will be regularly reviewing its parts to be certain that you are happy with its development and progress. To stay focussed will be an important part to ensure success.

Perhaps the initial creative work still needs to be done by you but you now know how to go about it. Afterwards you will find that you will be able to relax a little and allow the years to take their effect on the growth of your savings accounts, and that can be very rewarding. Just like planting a tree. A money tree!

But right now, your purpose should be to set some clear objectives for your retirement years. Some activities, pastimes or meaningful events that you want to do such as golf, sail, play your favourite sport such as tennis or swimming or go for trips and exotic vacations. Write down all of the things you want to do in your retirement years and then try to put some costs beside each activity. This activity will help you to develop an estimate as to how much you will need to live out your dream.

You may find that your goals are too expensive and that you may have to review your options somewhat. But that's o.k. too. Just do the exercise so as to have an approximate idea as to the cost of your leisurely pursuits. Then you can add on the costs for your everyday expenses such as your home, food, cars etc.

The objectives for retirement age must be practical, achievable and realistic. There is no point in setting your sights too high and being disappointed due to the fact that they never materialize. Remember, you have twenty years or so in which to manage your Retirement Plan and grow your money-tree so as to successfully accomplish your objectives.

"But twenty years seems too long a period in which to set realistic goals," I hear you say. In many respects, you are right. It's like the little boy who was told to eat the large piece of cake.

"But Mom, that's far too big for me to eat," he said protesting. His mother looked at him kindly and said,

"Of course it is dear. Let me cut it into little bite-size squares for you." This she did and Billy ate the whole thing!

Another important task is to create a Retirement Plan that is workable for you. As we are all different, it may be that you would feel happier with the idea of making regular minor adjustments as the years go along and your circumstances change. This seems entirely the right thing to do for we certainly want the project to be interesting, fun and rewarding. And I can tell you that it can be all of these!

So let's review what we have agreed. Here comes that list again.

You are to think about how you want to spend your retirement.

Jot down a list the activities you want to participate in.

Put a cost beside each one. Your best guess will be good enough at this time.

Include the fact that you will need to be debt free. Remember, being debt free means that you will not need so much income. This could slot you into a lower scale for income tax purposes.

Fine. Add anything else you feel is appropriate at this point. Perhaps you could do that part now.

You should certainly identify the debts that you presently have but are planning not to have in retirement. This is a very good point and has more benefits that you may at first realize.

Your sheet of paper could have a line drawn down the middle and on the left hand side of the page you could make a list of all your current debts in point form one under the other. Your list may look something like this:

Mortgage: $120,000
Car loan: $18,500
Another car loan: $10,000
Furniture store loan: $3,000
Another store loan: $2,500
Credit card: payments: $7,000
Another credit card: payments: $4,000
Bank loan or Line of Credit: $15,000

Total value of the current outstanding debt: $180,000.

Your monthly payment list may look something like this:
Mortgage: $120,000 - $890
Car loan: $18,500 - $350
Another car loan: $10,000-$175
Furniture store loan: $3,000 - $50
Another store loan: $2,500 - $50
Credit card: payments: $7,000 - $200
Another credit card: payments: $4,000 - $150

Bank loan or Line of Credit: $15,000 – $150

Current value of the monthly payments: $2,015

Remember that these items are the debts that you owe and the monthly payments that you incur because of the debts. There will of course be other monthly expenses.

Your additional monthly expenses will include the costs necessary to cover the operation of the house, the car, the boat, the cottage or any other daily or weekly expense for the family. These have not yet been accounted for. Such a list may look like this:

Food

Gasoline

Home Heating

Home water

Home Electricity

Property taxes

Toll road costs

Car service costs

Telephone

Cell phone (s)

Bottled water (home delivery)

Newspapers

Cottage: Mortgage and operating costs

Insurance: Home, cars and travel

Beer, wine and liquor

Pet foods and Veterinarian fees

Books, comics and toys

Lottery tickets

Daily expenses at work such as morning coffee, lunch, etc

Birthdays and special events gifts for family & friends

Dental and medical costs

Computer ink cartridges and paper

Sports equipment for the kids

Entertainment for the adults, movies, casino, etc

Vacation costs and spending money

How are you feeling? Well, now that you've picked yourself up off the floor, why don't we talk about these items? If you like we can group these costs and call them "Living costs." Or perhaps I should say "The cost of living!"

The cost of living these days is no doubt expensive for all of us and if you ever doubted that then perhaps I have just provided the proof that you needed. You see, you're really no different from nearly everyone else. This is why the banks make so much money, why the credit card companies make so much money and why that esteemed Canadian Gordon Sinclair observed in his wisdom many years ago. "It is wiser to EARN interest than to PAY interest."

But I want you to take another look at the lists above and truthfully answer this question. "How much do you need to earn to pay for all that you have listed?"

Absolutely. And in addition, ask yourself, "Are all of these costs necessary?" Perhaps this question is even more important.

You probably feel that most of the items are essential and if you are in a family situation maybe you should try putting the question to other family members. They'll soon tell you. But if you are living alone, then you have a better opportunity to reduce the list to bare minimums if you choose to. You and you alone are in sole charge of what you spend and so you are well able to lessen the monthly load by reducing your outgoings.

Any money saved could be added to your nest egg each month. Over a period of twenty years the savings that this single act could generate might run in to many tens of thousands of dollars. Rich in retirement suddenly becomes a reality.

This cost cutting exercise would seem to be a sensible option for couples to choose when they become "Empty Nesters", probably ten or so years before they retire. Again, here is a golden opportunity that should not to be missed – the opportunity to immediately accelerate the growth of their savings accounts.

Now this is where it gets really interesting.

Polly and I were with Joan and Roy one evening and as usual Roy and I were discussing investment opportunities and our respective futures including our Retirement Plans. We did that with increased regularity as we got nearer and nearer to our fifties and sixties. By that time, I not only had a retirement plan fully in place but I tracked it pretty well every week and felt that I really had my finger on the pulse so to speak.

However, there is a peculiar occurrence that takes place at about this point in your Retirement Plan and it is kind of strange.

In the days and months that the investment analysts refer to as "Bullish", you get all fired up and can't wait to check your investment funds on a very frequent basis. You just get so excited to see your savings growing so quickly, knowing that within a government sponsored tax sheltered fund, all of the growth is of course be tax-free. (Until you collapse it or withdraw increments.)

A very important part of this Retirement Plan is that during your high earning years you make every effort to pay off your debts. Then, when you need to collapse your tax-sheltered funds and receive some of your savings, you will only pay the minimum amount of income tax necessary by law. This is paramount to the success of the plan and so I stress this point on several occasions throughout the book.

During your retirement years you do NOT want to be earning lots of money. All that income causes you to pay lots of income tax. This cannot happen if you are carrying major debts.

But I digress. On other days, when the fund managers are talking about the markets being "Bearish" they are really saying that any stock market related funds you have are actually reducing in value. Now you don't need me to tell you that this is bad news and so naturally, we don't want to hear it. And you won't because if you are like me, I just couldn't get excited during those times. I reviewed my portfolio less regularly, just enough to stay focused and to know what was going on.

Those disappointing periods can continue on for several months if not years. However, do not despair. What goes down will come up again and remember, every cloud has a silver lining. For example, if the fund values are lower, there are opportunities to purchase bargains in the market place. (That is another reason for maintaining about 10% of your savings in some form of cash.) Also of course, the Bullish times can go on for years too and that is the good news.

It is important to always be aware of what is happening in the markets in other parts of the world from where you live too. In particular, major growth can suddenly occur in some of the poorer regions of the globe. You might have heard of the emerging markets. Business and economic news breaks at any time of the day and night and comes from every corner of the globe.

For the past twenty-five years or so, whenever I saw a newspaper article reporting what was going on in the markets I would read it fully, and a second time if necessary until I had a real grasp as to what the writer was saying. I knew that my retirement plan could be affected by it. I learned lots. About mortgages, investment schemes, compounding, investment trusts, stocks, shares, double up and double down. The information just never seemed to stop.

Anyway, back to Roy. We were discussing the plight of pensioners, trying to manage on one pot of money without the possibility of any additional earned income, in theory at least.

"But we'll still have to pay income tax on what we earn, even if it is only our pension won't we Robert?' Roy asked.

"Yes, of course we will, Roy," I replied. "But the trick will be to stay in the lower tax band."

"How do you mean, Robert?"

"Well, Roy. I figure that if we only receive the state pension with perhaps a little more from our savings, then it may well be possible to stay in the lower tax band for years which means that we would always pay income tax at the lowest possible level." "After all Roy," I continued, "If we can pay the minimum income tax we will be saving a bundle, and as our federal pensions may not be too much that would seem to make sense too don't you think?"

"Yes I agree." said Roy. "But how will you pay your mortgage, car payments and other loans if you don't have much income?"

"Well, I think that the trick is not to have any loans."

"What? Not to have any debt Robert? How would you buy a car for instance?"

"Pay cash Roy." "You see, if you have no mortgage and no loans whatsoever, then your income doesn't need to be very much and that way you remain in the lower tax band won't pay very much in income tax."

Roy sat up. "So really Robert, what you are saying is that we need to have our mortgage paid off by the time we retire."

"Right Roy! Debt free at 65, in the ideal world anyway, but if I am a year or two late I won't panic. That is what I am definitely planning."

"Also, it is my intention to have enough savings either in government sponsored tax sheltered funds or elsewhere so that I can afford to pay cash for everything. That way, I wont have a need for loans and the monthly payments that go with them." "And of course, by not having any payments, I will be avoiding paying any high interest rates. More savings for Polly and me and the money saved is all tax-free. Our monthly pensions should be able to cover almost everything apart from perhaps annual vacations."

"I think I need to adjust my retirement plan." Roy admitted.

And so, here again is the important lesson learned from that late night discussion.

You should plan to need as little monthly income as possible for when you retire. That way you will pay out less money in taxes. In the meantime, ...you will need to work very hard at having *no debts* left at the point when you do retire!

Remember. If you pay higher taxes, then you need to earn more money to pay the taxes and so it goes on. Try to stay in the lower income tax bands and save your money.

The good news for some of you is that when you retire, you may not have a high income! Indeed, you may not even have the opportunity to create any additional income, extra to any government pensions that you might be entitled to.

And so, at the risk of repeating myself, my tip to you is:

You must have NO debts when you retire! I think perhaps now you are beginning to get the picture, as they say!

Now, for the purpose of conducting this next exercise, I want you to imagine your retirement plan as a twenty-year segment of your life starting at age 45. At this point, it does not matter what your age is but we need to start somewhere.

Also, if we work on a 20-year schedule it will mature at the point when you become 65, just right for retirement. Again, the actual age when you retire at this point does not matter.

Next, to make it easier to understand I want you to break the 20-year span into four equal size slices and each of these will be a 5-year segment.

Take a look at the Mortgage Plan example in this chapter. The first thing that you will likely notice is its simplicity. Most people like to use the "KISS method when explaining financial related information. Keep It Simple Stupid! K.I.S.S.

You will see that the twenty-year projection grid is divided into four – five-year segments. As already stated, this is for ease of reference and allows the total plan to fit neatly on one page. If you are setting it up on a spreadsheet for your personal use, you can download it from WWW.RobertKite.net. You may perhaps want to extend the plan so that it appears on the worksheet as one complete grid.

The amortized period is 20 years. The word *"amortized"* comes from the French word "mort", to die or dead. If you like, during the 20-year period the mortgage will be dying and at year 20 it will be dead. And won't you be happy?

Do not confuse the amortized period with the *"Term"* of the mortgage. In some countries the expressions differ slightly but generally, the term of the mortgage will be the time period for which the mortgage is arranged. This might be for three years or five years or even ten years. In some circumstances the Term might even be for twenty years.

To repeat, the Term is the period of time covered by the present mortgage details. The Amortized period is the number of years that is used to work out the payments. This could be any period up to 25 or even 30-years.

I have set the amount of the mortgage owing at $130,000. This will be the principal. The interest rate is set at 6 %.

The total *interest* charged by the lender is approximately $94,000.00. You will be paying it over a period of 20-years and that makes it easier to manage.

But that is only the interest remember and for our purpose, it is assumed that the rate will be 6% per year. You will also need to repay the loan amount and that is another $130,000.

The total payments you will make to the lender in order to borrow $130,000 will amount to around $225,000. That's about $94,000 for the interest and $130,000 for the principal. Together they add up to about $225,000. Just imagine the money you would save if you didn't need a mortgage. Also, when you buy a house for say, $450,000 and you need a mortgage for $200,000, by the time you have paid the interest on the loan, the total house cost would amount to around $600,000!

But back to your plan. You will note that Year 0 is the year in which you arrange and take out the mortgage and commence your payments. Year One becomes the second year in which you continue paying down the mortgage. Year Two is the third year in which you are paying down the mortgage and so on. For your ease of reference, your projected age is already on the plan. It was the plan that I used to plot our retirement and I have to say that it worked well for Polly and me. Remember, the plan is only an example but it works well to illustrate the route you need to take during the course of your mortgage payments.

I have used the figure of $130,000 as the value of the mortgage. This is only a random amount. In your particular case it may be more or it may be less. Whatever the present value of your mortgage, divide it by the number of years remaining until you reach the age of 65. This gives you the amount you need to pay annually so as to ensure that you have no mortgage payments left at your retirement date. Your mortgage lender should be pleased to assist you to make the calculations.

There are a number of benefits for devising such a plan. Firstly it makes an excellent monitoring devise. As you will prepare the plan yourself you will be able to create it in such a way that you will easily understand it. As you enter the figures transposed from your mortgage papers that you received from the lender, the act of writing them down or keying them into a spreadsheet will help to fix them into your mind. Once completed, you then can print it and maintain a readily transportable document containing all the relevant information regarding your mortgage details including your personal schedule of planned payments and any extra payments that you hope to make.

IMPORTANT POINT

EXTRA PAYMENTS
MAKE YOUR MORTGAGE DISAPPEAR
SOONER

and

THEY SAVE YOU THOUSANDS OF $$$

Another use for the Mortgage Plan is to have a comparison chart so as to check your figures monthly or annually with the records that you receive from your mortgage lender. Financial institutions are not infallible and occasionally make mistakes. You may have already discovered this. Anyway, whenever your lender sends you any documents you will be able to double-check their accuracy with your newly made personal Mortgage Plan.

One further use for the Mortgage Plan is this. The figures that you use when you prepare it will come from the documents supplied to you by your mortgage lender. Depending on the Term of the mortgage, a period of time will pass without much happening by way of a change. Unless of course you force that change by having an "open" mortgage or the type of mortgage already discussed elsewhere in the book.

To confirm - the "open" Mortgage is the type of mortgage where you can make additional or extra payments every few months or every year. Whatever you have agreed with the mortgage lender. Under certain conditions, those extra payments that you are able to make will change the balance that you owe and so will also change the amount of interest that you will have to pay over the life of the mortgage.

When you compare the original Mortgage Plan that you prepared with the new values of the mortgage that you owe, especially after a few years, you may just get really excited to see in black and white, the great savings that you are beginning to make by making those extra payments. Talk with your mortgage lender or bank officer. They can show you exactly how your extra payments can make so much difference.

O.K. If you now have your mortgage papers in front of you, prepare a Mortgage Plan for yourself. This is just the start of many years of pleasure. You will feel in control and enjoy the moments as the years go by. But remember this. When it is time to re-negotiate the mortgage, read again the pages that deal with arranging a mortgage. While mortgages may all *look* the same, they may not all *BE* the same. Think about the type of mortgage that you want and go shopping. It will be a few years before you have this opportunity again.

Chapter Eight
Retirement Years. How do I get there?

This chapter will take you through the rudiments of getting from here to there, but before we can do that we need to know what we mean by there.

We know that "here" is where you are in our life right now. A snapshot if you like of you, frozen in time at this very point today. You, with all of your baggage that you have including your assets, your liabilities which include you debts, your job, your income, your monthly payments, your marital status (I think they call it), in fact everything that is you.

The "there" that I am referring to is the position that you want to be in when you are finished with your full time job. So, it is now for me to explain clearly to you how you can get yourself from here to there.

As we need to use a future age for the purpose of discussion, let us assume that we are happy to peg our preferred age of retirement at sixty-five. To know the actual age is unnecessary at this point but to allow us to do some number crunching we need to put something on paper.

Also, at this point, we need to think about how much money we will need when we are sixty-five. All sorts of figures are suggested. I have heard "eighty percent of salary" mentioned. I have also heard "sixty percent of salary." Another theory I have heard is that the full amount of the Canadian CPP and the Old Age Security will provide about 40% of a retirement income for the average person, and so the balance of sixty-percent must presumably come from a private pension fund. But if you did the exercise in the last chapter you will already have calculated your financial needs at retirement.

Polly and I were going shopping the other day and we met a recently retired neighbour in the elevator. Polly asked her how she was enjoying her new found free time.

"You know Polly, it's amazing. Now that I am retired, it costs me so little to live on."

"Really." answered Polly, almost disbelievingly.

"Yes," continued MaryAnne. "I realize that I am single but I don't seem to spend half as much as I did when I was working."

"Why do you think that is?" asked Polly.

"I'm not sure, Polly but now that I think about it, I guess I don't run my car as much as I did, and I don't use as many dressy clothes as I used to when I was in business. I don't buy so many lunches during the week either."

"I suppose not," commented Polly.

MaryAnne continued, "I often wondered how things would work out for me when I was retired, but now that I am here, I seem to be better off than I ever was." We both felt happy for her as we said goodbye.

And isn't that marvellous news, because when we are working, I suppose that we all have that same concern, especially when we are nearing retirement.

That brief conversation had me thinking about that old thought that, "Two people can live as cheaply as one." Well that may be fine during our working life, but how does that equate to a retirement situation? It can mean quite a lot of different things to different people. You see, only last week I was talking to another of Polly's friends. Janet lives by herself in a one-bedroom apartment. It is very cosy, well decorated and in a quiet residential area. The apartment is a little on the small side for her needs as Janet sometimes has her grandchildren visit her and they like to stay over on the weekends.

She has her CPP and Old Age Security pensions and she also has some extra income that she earns by taking part in clinical tests at a local medical centre. She loves dancing and is frequently seen at tea dancing events at a local arena.

"How do you find things Janet?" I inquired.

"Oh, just fine Robert." My income from pensions and other sources is not very much but I get by."

"Do you still have your car?" I inquired.

"No, I needed to sell that." replied Janet. "The repairs were starting to cost me a fortune." "Also, the running costs were very expensive now that the price of gas has gone up again."

"It must be difficult Janet," I commented.

"It is a bit, but I find public transportation very good where I live and if I am travelling when it is dark, I usually get a cab." answered Janet

"That seems a very good idea Janet," I agreed. "Safe too."

"I pay a small rent here where I live and each month I have a little over for goodies for the grandchildren." "You know what they are like," she continued. "Always wanting to go to the movies or somewhere."

"Yes," I replied. "I suppose it can't be too easy with just the one income."

"That's right," she said. If Joe was still alive, then there would be two incomes like there used to be."

"Did that make things easier Janet?" I asked.

"Oh yes, Robert." "A lot easier."

I decided to push a bit further. "In what way?"

"Well, you know." Two CPP pensions, two Old Age security Pensions, plus Joe had a small works pension from his firm." "After all, he was there for sixteen years and so he deserved that."

Janet thought for a moment and then she said, "And of course, Joe also used to help out at the local bar. You know, helping with the stocking up of the shelves and washing glasses. Although, to be honest Robert, I don't really know what he did but he always enjoyed going down there each day." "Joe always said that it wasn't like work, and they were very kind to him."

"Do you know that on a Sunday, after they had served the customers, they used to give Joe his lunchtime meal?"

"Well that was very nice for him Janet," I interrupted.

"Yes, and they gave him a beer with it too." "All that pleasure that he had and then every second Friday, they gave him his wages." "Joe used to joke with me sometimes saying that he would have gone there and helped out for nothing."

"Well Janet, I guess he obviously enjoyed it," I added.

"That's what I am saying," Janet went on. "The extra cost for Joe to live here with me was negligible. He didn't eat much, and he never spent money on clothes or anything." "No, the only extra cost was the car and when we went on a vacation."

I thought of the old chestnut. "So what you are saying Janet, is that two could live as cheaply as one."

"Exactly Robert!" "You've hit the nail right on the head." She chuckled.

Well, two might well be able to live as cheaply as one, but then why do I sometimes hear that we need to have about five times our final-year annual income saved in RRSP's by the time we are sixty-five?

I am sure that you will agree that this is all very confusing. That is why it is important to separate some of the numbers so that a sensible calculation can be made. Hopefully, you have now done that.

But let's stay with this thought and see if the official numbers calculate similarly to our own ones.

Again, the final dollar figure we will use for this example is academic but we need to use something. Perhaps if we take a little of all the suggestions and add something for a margin of safety we could use the figure of three times annual earnings in RRSP's at the retirement age of sixty-five.

Let's be clear. If for example, I was presently employed full time but about to retire, and my annual salary was $70,000, I multiply this by 3 and that is the minimum as a lump sum I would need in my nest egg. As this is estimated for each person, Polly and I would need to have a lump sum of $420,000 as our money tree.

There are a couple of points to remember here. Firstly, at retirement, there will be two C.P.P. pensions coming in to the family pot in addition to the Old Age Security income if we qualify.

Next. One or both of us may have a small pension to come from our former employer. In addition, we may have a small income from a LIF. When we reach 71, under the present Canadian law we will each be required to withdraw some of our tax sheltered RRIF funds.

All of this income, while our nest egg of $420,000 has remained untouched until now. It has changed though because it has been earning interest and at 4%, it earned $16,800 in the first year.

So, however much you as an individual earn each year, project it forward to your retirement age. You will need to guess here a bit, then multiply the amount by three. You may be shocked and think that you cannot possibly live on that. Well, just relax because as I have just shown you, things will likely be better for you than you think.

As was pointed out in the exercise, when you retire there can be several sources of income. Lets review them.

1. You have every hope of receiving a C.P.P. pension.
2. You may qualify to receive an Old Age Security income.
3. You may qualify to receive a Guaranteed Income Supplement. [G.I.S.].
4. You may receive a private pension that you have been paying into.
5. You may qualify to receive a pension from any companies that you had been working for.

In addition to the above, there may be other pension plans for which you qualify and so you may be surprised as to how much in dollars your pensions all add up to.

Also, if you have saved some RRSP's in a tax sheltered fund, and have managed to accumulate a dollar amount that is three times your final salary it is unlikely that you will need to start drawing that immediately you retire.

You may well find yourself interested to find some form of part-time employment. If so then the income will help to supplement your pensions and all of these incomes will help put off the day you need to draw on your RRSP retirement fund. This has two distinct advantages.

1. The later you are in life before you need to draw on your RRSP or RRIF retirement fund, the longer it is likely to last you.

2. For every year that you can leave your RRSP retirement fund untouched, the greater the amount to grow. The growth will vary of course according to the type of investment and the level of risk.

As a rule of thumb, the older you are, the lower the level of risk. This is the reason:

Let us say that you are in your thirties or early forties and at that time you have some savings in an RRSP fund. You should always diversify your portfolio, but that notwithstanding, at that time in your life, should you so wish, you probably could afford to take a higher risk. The reason is that if a catastrophe happened and you lost a large proportion of the fund, you would have many years ahead of you for the fund to recover and grow.

However, should such an event happen to you when you are in your sixties or seventies, you do not have the necessary number of years available to make a good recovery.

MONTHLY BUDGETING MADE EASY

– From little acorns big oak trees grow.

The whole purpose of you reading this book is to learn how to assemble lots of money, save it and allow the years ahead of you to grow your pile large enough to have a good time when you retire. That is putting it very simply.

As Julie Andrews sings in The Sound of Music, "Nothing comes from Nothing," and the sentence above makes it very clear what the most important aspect of your project will be if you are to achieve your goal. Yes. The key phrase is, "to assemble lots of money."

It is logical therefore that we need to discuss something as basic as monthly budgeting. You know, keeping a track of how much you spend on all of the items that you buy each month. You probably don't work to a budget at the moment and that's fine because most people that I have spoken to don't either.

It is a good idea to start a budget, especially if you are really serious about planning for your later years and you want to enjoy a happy, worry free retirement. This is known as taking responsibility. You need to be accountable for the actions that you take and if you overspend, you need to know it and you need to know by how much so that you can take appropriate action and hopefully take that new found experience into the future months and cease overspending immediately.

To continue overspending will put your retirement plan in jeopardy and you should not take that risk.

You no doubt know that we all spend too much money on unnecessary things. This is a modern habit that everyone is guilty of. The difference is that some people can afford it and they are probably not looking to save money for the future, especially if they are already there. But if you are younger than fifty then I seriously encourage you to prepare a budget immediately, so that it is ready to begin on the first day of next month. You will find it interesting to see exactly where your money goes.

Refer to the Monthly Budget Grid that I have included in the book. There are a few tips here too, as you might have guessed.

Personalise the headings at the top of the columns appropriate to your particular needs.

Carry the amounts forward each month so that you can keep a running total as you go.

If there are several members in your family then a separate grid for each one might be a good idea. If this is too tiresome, make a separate column for each person with a heading entitled *Personal* and their initials.

Make sure that every expense is recorded. Even the smallest costs add up over the months and may put you completely off track.

Encourage all the members of the family to submit receipts to you. Tell them that this is for a trial period of two weeks. That may be long enough for them to get the habit.

Record the information on a daily basis. To leave a pile on the table an plan to do it weekly will not work. The pile grows quickly and you will be depressed and discouraged just to look at it.

Do it. You may just enjoy it. If the other members of the family don't want to join in then go it alone.

You will probably find it a lot easier than you think, especially if you are diligent and charge the particular item that you bought to the proper budget.

Refer to the Monthly Budget plan to help you but remember, as it is only an example, the estimated costs are strictly fictitious. It will be up to you to create your own chart, using your own cost estimates. You can do it!

All of this work will help you get to where you want to be. Financially secure in your retirement.

Chapter Nine
A SMOOTH PATH OR A ROCKY ROAD
What are the hidden dangers?

Like any smooth lake or quiet backwater, there may always be possible dangers lurking beneath the surface. But should we be afraid? Not really. But we should be wary and extremely cautious. A smart part of the adventure is to try to be prepared by reviewing the potential difficulties so that you know what signs or signals to look for. Of course, this is easy to say but like any situation, it is really only experience and information that can prepare you for the unexpected.

The experience will come as the years unfold and you watch your Retirement Plan prosper. Because you have a Retirement or Financial Plan, you will probably find yourself more interested in the general happenings in the world and especially anything to do with economics with Canadian connections.

You will find yourself distracted in a conversation or when you are driving. The moment that something is talked about that might affect your savings you turn up the volume not wishing to miss a word. You may even find yourself more interested in the Dow Jones index, the NASDAQ and the Toronto Stock Exchange (TSX) indices. All this will provide you with a valuable experience so that you can be one step ahead when you next see your financial advisor.

The information will come from a variety of sources. Most of us hear things on the news every day that might affect our savings.

Recently my friend Bob asked me if I had heard the latest?

"What's that Bob?" I asked.

"Well, the Government is reviewing the arrangements for Investment Trusts and it is said that they might be making some changes."

"My ears immediately pricked up. "Oh really?" I asked, knowing that anything to do with investments and in particular, government legislation, could very easily have an effect on our savings.

It could also affect the value of the Canadian dollar on the currency exchanges around the world. In turn, this could affect the cost of Canadian manufactured goods and services and have a major downturn in the overall economy for the Country. A slight exaggeration perhaps but as they say, anything is possible.

Small wars break out all over the world, displacing people and creating havoc among the cities where it happens. This may create jobs and business for people who make bombs and ammunition but it also may affect the oil stocks that are held across the globe. In turn, this could cause the price of oil to rise or fall, having an immediate affect on transportation and the price of shipping goods around the world.

With global warming among us, the world is changing almost everywhere, and with an increase in forest fires and floods, the price of timber and paper is also affected. This has a ripple effect on the cost of houses, furniture, packing cases and other materials, all causing world prices to fluctuate.

People worry about the weather and perhaps cancel cruises and other holiday trips. The travel and tourism industry is affected and again we see people losing jobs and hotels closing down. Fortunately, the news is not usually as severe as this but it only takes one or two disasters to occur and the markets are in turmoil.

These are just some of the dangers to look out for. But, as they say, it is an ill wind that blows nobody any good. If the value of savings starts to drop there is the possibility that you may wish to capitalize on the situation and scoop up some bargains. By the way, bargains in this sense could be good stocks that have recently seen their values fall. This may be a temporary blip and the smart people buy these stocks at the undervalued prices. Hence, they are bargains.

Even the Blue Chip funds can lose their values during tough times and these too can be bought at discount prices.

Other dangers may come from your own company pension fund. Always keep an open mind with any company or private pension fund that you might have. While the Directors may make all sorts of promises in good faith, things happen and changes are made with the best intentions for the sake of the company. Unfortunately, it is not always in the best interest of the individual and people like you and me have found their pension funds devalued overnight.

All sorts of guarantees are made and while the Directors of the fund have mean well, things happen and afterwards, excuses are made as to why decisions were made that caused the funds to lose their value.

Do not be naïve and assume that because things are said, that is how they will remain. Life is not like that and company directors have gone to prison for embezzlement and defrauding employees out of their pensions.

FOUR-YEAR EQUITY CYCLE

While we cannot foresee everything (unless we can use a crystal ball successfully) we should do some advanced homework to better inform ourselves of some of the pitfalls and to learn of the opportunities that might present themselves when disaster strikes.

Here is an example, and this is really interesting. During the past fifty years, the economy in the U.S. has taken a correction every four years almost without exception. And if it doesn't happen in the fourth then it will almost certainly occur in the fifth year.

Correction is a smooth word, but what it really means is that almost all of the markets took a significant drop in dollar value. I alert you to this because as you may already know, any major shift in the U.S. stock market will almost certainly affect Canadian equities as well as the rest of the world.

As many Canadian mutual funds contain a percentage of U.S. stocks then these can expect to be devalued as a result of the U.S. stock market "correction."

This is very concerning and any news like this should get your attention immediately you hear about it. They call it a "U.S. Equity Cycle." To an average investor in Canada the results can be quite alarming especially if they are unprepared for such an announcement. Immediately the effect to the international marketplace and global investment houses seems to be a total calamity.

Terror strikes in the heart of many fund managers too. Bad news never makes a good day for them. However, what comes down must go up and so the good news is that a boom for two years will almost always follow a year in which there is a major correction.

The professional people in the know recommend that we stay the course and retain our investments with the result that in time, the funds will recover to their earlier high values and then continue to appreciate from that point forward.

IMPORTANT POINT

WHEN THERE IS A CORRECTION

AND FUND VALUES CRASH

BE THE SMART ONE

CONSIDER STAYING WITH IT... AND

HOLD OUT FOR THE LONG TERM GAIN

If you decide to sell your mutual funds when the global markets take a dive, you will only be cashing in your losses. Remember that your losses are only on paper and are not actual losses unless you sell them. The major point here is to remind yourself that you are in the investment business for the long term and so be strong and brave. Keep your funds, focus on your long-term goals and in time, the fund values will return and you should prosper.

It is very much hoped that the day when the markets are hit with a correction you are within reach of your fund manager for there could be some work for you to do. Disaster Recovery. Hopefully this will not be your disaster but perhaps you might want to have a hand in the recovery.

This is where the mature investors enter the scene. They stroll in with a casual but confident air about them, they sniff around and consider the bouquet as if they were deciding on a vintage wine, and then they strike, for there are bargains to be snapped up. Yes, this is pay off day and while I am not suggesting that you buy just anything on offer, I would be remiss if I were to advise you not to review the re-valued fund prices compared with their previous values.

If your fund manager agrees that it's a good idea then you might decide to see what's on offer and buy a few funds at their re-valued low prices. That is why it is important to maintain at least ten percent of your portfolio in cash or bonds. With your liquid assets on hand you will have the cash to join the bargain hunt.

I am told that there are few things that provide the level of satisfaction as the feeling of walking in and picking up the pieces, buying some good quality stocks at bargain-basement prices after others have panicked and cashed in their losses.

Another hidden danger is to assume too much.

IMPORTANT POINT

PLANNING TO RETIRE BEFORE 65 IS O.K.

BUT C.P.P., Q.P.P. AND OTHER PENSIONS

USUALLY START MUCH LATER!

Let us suppose that you wish to retire before 65. Maybe you are forecasting your retirement age to be 63 or even 60. To coincide with this you would perhaps then also plan to be debt free at the same time like I did.

Your budget calculations will include the forecast for Income. Be careful that you do not fall into the trap of including your state pensions such as your CPP and your Old Age Security pension. Unfortunately, they don't start arriving until a few years later.

That is why a chart is vital and makes planning so much easier. If you make all the correct calculations the figures will announce to you if you can afford to retire full time and so you will avoid what could be a large disappointment.

WHAT IS THE PAIN?

If you find the realization daunting that perhaps nobody wants to employ you after you are 60, then how about 55, or even 45? And when you think of the size of the mortgage that may still hang over you, stark panic might really start to set in. I know. I was there.

If this happens to you and you happen to be single at the time then the feeling of being totally dependant upon yourself can be very alarming. I can already hear you thinking, "Who needs to retire?" Perhaps I'd better hang on to that job." "Retirement? Well perhaps I never wanted to retire anyway!"

That would be quite a dilemma you would find yourself in either as a single or as a couple. Aged 50 and out of a job with a hefty mortgage to maintain and a new car you just leased for 4 years. What to do? You take a big breath, think long and hard and consider all of your options. Take out that large sheet of paper, draw a line down the middle and start writing.

Yes, we are talking of pain in this section of the book and there can be much of this along the path to a happy retirement.

It may even take days if not weeks to sort out a workable solution. I remember that in my particular case I was just 56, and yes, the week before, I had just taken delivery of a new car with bank repayments of $325 every month for three years. I had a mortgage of around $120,000 and no job. Fortunately Polly was working at that time and her monthly income just about covered the mortgage payment but things were very tight and we had to do some heavy thinking.

Over the next several weeks Polly and I had many discussions. Eventually we came to the conclusion that our options were in fact very limited. I was 56 and needed a job that would provide me with a reasonable income until I was 65. I certainly would not be able to consider just any job, as the salary would need to cover our every day expenses just in case Polly lost her job too. For me to be bringing in just an average wage could spell disaster. No. I would need to hold out for a position in my established field of work. It would need to be hotel or institutional management. I gave myself a year to find something.

Actually, it was four months and 167 job applications later when I landed one. I can't tell you how relieved we were when the joyous news came through. It was a good job with major responsibilities and an excellent salary with benefits. At my age, 56, I not only felt lucky, I felt grateful too. It was a very humbling experience to go through and one that I shall never forget.

That situation reminded me of an earlier experience when things went badly for me in my career. Not as badly as that, but rocky just the same.

We had been living in Canada for several years but as both Polly and I had family in the U.K., we continued to enjoy returning to visit them but the cost of this trip was increasing every year. In fact, I recall on one occasion when I was searching for flight fares being stunned by the high cost. Polly turned to me and confessed that she thought our days of trans-Atlantic travel were over for good.

My employment prospects were not good and in fact I even felt insecure in the job that I had at that time. I remember worrying about the future and wondered constantly about what would happen to us. What would we do if my job ended and our income trickled to a standstill?

It was about that time that I sat down in our study and decided that we needed a financial plan to take us from our present state to where we needed to be in twenty-years time.

A feasible plan, that if followed would guide us from our present point to where we wanted to be, say, when we retired. I asked Polly what her expectations were for our retirement years. As would be the case with many people, Polly told me that she could not think that far ahead.

I decided on quietly going about it myself. I prepared a chart and divided it with twenty, one-year segments. I then put five of the one-year segments together, which displayed four-five year columns. I figured that I would like to retire at sixty-five and so, as I was forty-five, the year when I would be sixty-five, became year TWENTY.

It was important in my mind that year TWENTY must be the last year in which I would be making any mortgage payments. Actually, in fact, it works out that year nineteen is the twentieth year, but that would provide me with a year's grace. But the actual year would be academic. The important thing was to nail down the fact that I should be debt free at 65. But there were other issues to consider carefully too. Let me explain.

I estimated that when I retired there would be certain "givens."

It would be a "given" that I would *not* be working.

It would be a "given" that my income would be considerably less than when I was working.

As I would be earning less, it was a "given" that I would be in a different tax bracket for income tax purposes and as such, I would be paying less income tax to the government.

As already mentioned elsewhere, these were all important points to consider in my plan. For if I wanted to qualify for a reduced income tax assessment then I would need to earn less. And yet, how could we survive if I was to earn less and continue to enjoy the same lifestyle and quality of life?

Answer: If we could reduce our monthly payments to pay off debts then our monthly living costs would reduce correspondingly.

Our monthly debt payments at that time consisted of :

a: mortgage

b: car payments

c: credit card payments.

If I could be sure that these did NOT exist when I retired then my only outgoings would be for accommodation, (such as condominium fees and taxes), food, car, clothes, entertainment and vacations. As the last three of these would be discretionary costs then why shouldn't this plan work?

The key to the plan's success would be to keep the expenses down so as to keep down the necessity for a high income. But would it work? What steps would need to be taken so as to eliminate the debts from the chart by year TWENTY.

It became clear that some more serious thought was necessary. I poured another cup of coffee, sharpened my pencil and got down to work.

The following week I made an appointment to see an employee with the bank.

"Can you show me how I can pay down the mortgage on our house sooner? I asked.

"Let us see" she said as she pulled out my file. "Ah Yes! You are paying a monthly mortgage with a term of five-years and a fixed rate amortised over twenty-five years. The mortgage is due next year which means that you will need to re-negotiate the set-up of the mortgage including the payment arrangement."

"I have been thinking." I started. "I have made some calculations. Given that the loan-interest is calculated monthly after each payment, it would appear that if I were able to make *weekly* payments rather than monthly payments, I could make some significant savings over the twenty-five year term." "Would you agree?"

"Yes, I would agree," she replied. I was pleased to hear this. "Except that the bank does not currently have any arrangement that includes that option."

"If I found a bank with that option, I suppose I would have to move lenders?" I asked.

"Yes, that is correct" she said. "But of course, the bank would not wish to lose you as a customer."

"I see," I replied. I thought for a moment, leaving the silence available so that she could make any proposal necessary so as to retain my business. After a few moments she closed the file and looked me in the eye.

"Mr. Kite," she said. "I don't know what else I can suggest. I know that we would not like to lose your business. If you feel there are other options that you would like to put forward then I know that we would be pleased to consider them."

"Well, I do have another idea," I responded. "As you have said that the bank wouldn't allow me to make *weekly* payments, do you think that the bank would you permit me to make *additional* payments, over and above the regular monthly payments?" "You see," I continued. "if I was permitted to make three or four *extra* payments each year and after each payment, the interest remaining was re-calculated on the revised balance, it would have the same effect of reducing the balance of the loan, thus creating considerable savings on the amount of interest, wouldn't it?."

She thought for a while.

"Yes, it would." She continued. "Perhaps not exactly, but certainly I can see how savings on the interest would accrue. This would produce the result that at the end of each annual anniversary of the mortgage, you would have money in you pocket, so to speak."

She smiled.

"Would you like me to inquire as to whether we can do that for you Mr. Kite?"

I looked at Polly for her approval and returned the smile to the bank employee.

"Yes please. We would be very grateful if you could check on that and indeed, any other options that may save us interest on the renewed mortgage."

Polly and I left the bank and went for a coffee to consider what we would want to do if the bank agreed with our request.

"Darling, don't you think that we should pursue other options too," Polly asked.

"Yes Polly, I do. And it's a good idea that you mentioned it." I took another sip of my Latte.

"Polly, do you think that while we are here in the Shopping Mall, we should take the opportunity to go and visit some other banks and see just what they are offering? That way we can consider *all* of the options before we sign on the dotted line." I continued, "Time is on our side Polly and remember that sometimes, no decision is the best decision."

Polly agreed. We felt happy that we were thinking along the same lines and she snuck her arm in mine as we set off to look around and to consider all of the options. This is an important point to remember when considering any purchase.

On that day we were searching to purchase a mortgage as it happens, but whatever the purchase, it is always prudent to shop around and visit as many suppliers as possible. Compare prices, look carefully at any documentation and scrutinise the small print. If it is too small to read and to understand thoroughly then ask for an enlarged copy. The onus is on all of us as customers or consumers to know exactly what we are getting into before signing on the dotted line or parting with our money. The onus is on anyone who is selling something to clearly state what obligation the buyer is getting into prior to any exchange of money. Make sure that they do that.

If you think that you need time to think over the offer, then say so and walk away. Whatever it is that you are buying. If things don't sound entirely right or if you feel uncertain about something that the sales person has said, then do one of two things. Either ask questions until things are made clear to you or walk away. Tell the store associate that you need time to think about it. That is your prerogative.

NEGATIVE GROWTH

How about dealing with another related issue but something fairly simple? How do you feel when you save a few dollar bills? Do you fold them up and take them to the bank and invest them in your personal a savings account? I do. I have a sort of good feeling that in time they will grow and reward me with their new value. A bit like a flower really - You pop in the seeds, give them a little water occasionally and, watch out! Stand back. Here they come - beautiful flowers everywhere for you to admire for as long as you like. Well, that is the same feeling I get when I invest money. I imagine that it will grow and I will be delighted to stand back and admire the results.

With some savings plans such as a deposit account with a bank, the interest is added to the capital amount at the end of each year. Other arrangements provide for the interest to be paid daily, weekly, quarterly, (every three months) or at some other pre-arranged time, but for the sake of this exercise, we will use the annual type. And so the interest is regularly added to the capital amount - the original investment that you made.

At the end of the second year, the interest is added to the combined investment, made up of the original savings and the interest from the first year. And so it goes on. The rewards are there to see. But more than just in monetary terms, the growth is there, every year. As sure as the sun comes up every morning.

Personal savings plans offered by banks will always pay you interest for depositing your money with them.

The procedure with investment and mutual fund is similar in that you earn interest on your savings. THERE THE SIMILARITY ENDS.

Mutual funds and similar other forms of investments can earn interest and usually do earn interest. However there are times when they earn nothing. Also, there are times when they lose their value. I repeat, YOUR INVESTMENT HAS REDUCED IT'S VALUE. It is now worth LESS than when you first deposited it.

Here again is PAIN.

There is no interest, or at least, no interest as we have gotten to know it. Rather than grow, we discover that our flower of cash has wilted. Of course, the first thing we do is panic. We think of changing our financial adviser or at the very least, change our investments by throwing out some funds and trading others for something more attractive.

But just because we have been provided with a different result shouldn't give us cause to make poor judgement decisions. We will not feel good about the situation that's for sure, in fact we will feel very disappointed. But what we are looking at here is what is known as *negative interest*. It happens sometimes and now, on this occasion it is staring us right in the face.

Occasionally, it might occur in several months. If the number of months is more than the months when our flower was earning interest, then the year-end result would be that of negative interest. Nothing earned by our invested money for the entire year! This is extremely disappointing for everyone, and in particular, for the people who work as stockbrokers. Frequently the level of their pay-check is commensurate with the level of the stock values that they manage.

So get used to the idea that some years may produce a negative interest on your savings. We don't like it of course, but it is not all bad. After all, when stocks and shares go right down to the bottom, where else can they go?

Yes. The happy news is that they will return to the values that we once enjoyed not so long ago.

Remember, as discussed earlier, the important lesson here is that we should not be tempted to change horses in mid-stream. Just because your investments have devalued is no reason to sell them or to trade them in for something else. Remember too that if you sell your investments when they have fallen in value, you will be cashing in your losses.

They have only lost their value on paper and when they bounce back in value, so will your savings. The net result for you will be a happy return to positive interest days along with any stocks that you bought for the bargain prices that availed themselves during the months of the correction. I repeat. If you fall to temptation and cash them in you will only be realising the losses and take the hit, full in the stomach, or should I say, full in the pocket book.

And so, as well as the good times, these painful times are the days when investors like you and I just have to accept what is given to us and acknowledge that this is all part of the joy if investing for the long term. Certainly, we get disgruntled with our investments and with our investment advisers too, and this is entirely understandable. If we want the gain, I suppose we have to take the pain.

TOUGH AS A COUPLE? TRY BEING A SINGLE

I am sure that we all agree that whether we are a single parent or a couple with one of you at home full time, trying to pay for all the necessities of a home life while also saving for a retirement is a very difficult thing to do when living on one paycheque. It is one thing to prepare a personal Retirement Plan but to be able to stay the course, dig in and fight off the tough times so as to see your objectives come true really takes some doing.

There is no question that with just the one income coming in, you will need to make trade offs and this is where it gets really tricky. If you think that you are already living on a tight budget, then you need to know that those strings are about to be pulled even tighter.

Here are some suggestions to help:

Who are you impressing anyway?

Who is guilty of paying a little over the top just to impress someone? You know, a larger house than we really need in an avenue of trees so that the family will be impressed when they come to visit us. Or two upscale cars in the driveway when we could probably manage on one lesser expensive model. And the cute thoroughbred pooch we bought from a breeder when we could have saved the life of a loveable hound-dog in the pound? And what about the expensive designer T-shirts we bought on the credit card when the ones in Old Navy looked just as good and we could have paid cash. Right?

Well this sort of decision-making is all wrong and you will need to get your head round the idea that spending in this way has to come to an immediate halt. It might be easier if you are a little older, say in your forties. You know what it is to have enjoyed the good times and really, they were not that hot were they?

So, with this new way of managing your money and your lifestyle, the dollars that you save now and put away in an investment plan will see you slide very happily into your retirement years the way you want to. And while you are cutting corners to save the dollars, you will enjoy every moment, knowing that you are building assets and not debts, which is just another word for liabilities. You will also feel very content when you meet your friends and see them spending money unnecessarily on things. You may even want to persuade them to adjust to your new thrifty way of living.

Some months ago, I was talking to Amber, a neighbour in her forties. She mentioned that this was the time of the year when she was filing her tax return. Suddenly, her face shone and she started to laugh.

"And guess what?" she asked me.

"I've no idea, Amber," I replied.

"I'm getting a tax refund this year and I'm going to put it into some savings for my retirement."

"Well, that seems a marvellous idea Amber," I answered. "It can't be easy living on a single income these days. I'm very happy for you. You should be proud of yourself."

"I sure am Robert," she said. "I thought about taking the cash and having a good time but I knew I would only blow it on something I didn't really need and so I decided to invest it for my old age." she added.

"You see Robert, I remember the discussion we had last year and how you impressed on me how important it was for me to save for my retirement."

She seemed really happy about her future prospects. She said that when she spoke to the tax office, she was advised that if she decided not to take the refund at this time, then the amount of tax deducted from her paycheque every two weeks could be reduced. "And with the extra money, that means that I can make contributions into an RRSP"

"But couldn't you just take the tax refund and invest it directly Amber?" I asked.

"Oh yes, I could. But I don't know if I would have the will power!"

Amber explained that she would almost certainly spend the cash before she had a chance to get to an investment adviser. I couldn't argue with that.

I understand that Amber is now making regular payments to an investment fund. She feels very happy that an investment fund has been set up specifically to provide her with a retirement pension, and it is doing just fine.

Good Luck to Amber. I think that she will do very well. If she sees this book she may even learn how to become debt free at 65.

IT'S O.K. TO SAY "NO" TO KIDS SOMETIMES

Kids. Who would do without them? We love them all. They are the little rays of sunshine in our lives from the time we get up to the time we go to bed. They are so all-powerful. All-powerful to make us happy, sad, and worried, even scared. And we want so much for them and we want to give them so much too.

Well that's fine, but as we say that, lets just take a look at some of the bills that they caused us during the past year or so.

There was the hockey outfit and then the running shoes that had to be the in-fashion statement, because, "All the other kids have 'em." Then along came springtime and a bike was the craze. But not just any

bike, a new one, "Just like the other guy's on the bock have, Mom."
Oh yes and then the skateboard. How much was that? And don't forget
about the protective apparel that they need to go with it. Well, we don't
want them to hurt themselves do we?

Look. We don't need to tell kids that the money has all gone
and the wealth-well has run dry. They just wouldn't understand.
Heaven knows, it's tough enough for us to understand. So, as this book
has not yet found its way into any classroom as part of the Personal
Financial Management 101 curriculum, you might just try this. Sit
down with them and teach them something about budgeting.

Explain that money really does *not* grow on trees, and that you
too need something that you are saving for. Tell your kids. Spell it out
for them. It is called retirement planning and if you are not allowed to
save enough money at this stage in your life, then how about telling
them that they will be keeping you in your old age. Kapeesh? You
might well get their attention.

Tell them that you want them to have everything possible but
that not everything will be possible. Unfortunately there can be trade-
offs. If they can't handle that then suggest to them that maybe they
should just start looking for a job. Something that will help them to pay
for their excesses over and above the standard things that you will of
course be happy to provide.

If you do this, you will be providing your children with a great
education. You will be giving them a lesson for life that they will be
teaching to their kids when their turn comes around. And don't forget
to hug them to bits and tell them how much you love them. You need
them in your life forever.

CARS CAN LAST LONGER THAN YOU THINK

I was all set to change my car this year. After all, the lease runs
out and so after four years, it is time for a change. Why not indulge
myself? Well that was exactly what I was going to do. The car we have
is a modest car but comfortable. It has lots of bells and whistles. Funny,
how your mind works when you decide to lease a car. Almost like you
are not paying for it and so why not have the leather seats and the
sunroof?

"Did you want the top of the line stereo system, Mr. Kite?" I hear the salesman ask. Well why not, I think to myself. After all, I'm not paying cash for it and over four years, an extra few thousand dollars will convert to only a few extra dollars each month. And so, we finished up leasing a small but luxury car.

Here we are, four years later, thinking about changing again, because we have had it for four years. Oh yes. I forgot to mention the kilometres that it has travelled. Just forty-one thousand. Kilometres not miles, and I am thinking of walking away from it as it is four years old. The buyout cost is modest and so after due consideration, it fits neatly into my current budget to cough-up the money needed so that we can call it our own.

The best part of course is that there will be no more monthly payments. You see, even though I am retired, I still have a five-year plan in place and in another three years my new five-year plan commences. I look forward to changing the car at that time. I also look forward to the happy feeling I will have as a result of all that money I will be saving.

And so, I am saying to you, during the remaining years of your working life, if you can control the urge to dash out and look at the new models when they arrive in the showroom, you too will be making lovely savings – savings that will roll over into retirement income when you are old enough to really need it.

When you consider all the benefits, it makes sense to keep your car for an extra two or three years.

You will have to get used to saying no to your indulgences. I did warn you that there would be times when it would hurt.

But as they say, "No pain, no gain."

IS DOWNSIZE THE ROUTE TO KING SIZE?

It has been said by many that the most important asset we have is our home. It is also true that the most expensive investment we ever make is *in* our home. You like where you live of course. Otherwise, why else would you have made the purchase? But take a moment. Take a moment and look around you. Your home might be everything that you ever needed. But is all of your home really what you need?

I am asking the question, because it is The Question that at this time in your life, you should be asking yourself. "O.k." I hear you answering.

"But this is truly a lovely home and I feel that it is perfect for our family, particularly at this time in our lives." you say.

Well fine. But how about downsizing. Whoops. Did I say something? No. Now c'mon, wait a minute. Before you just give up the idea, throw in the towel and throw out the book. Think about it. Is it so crazy?

Are you really getting a one hundred per-cent use from all of the space here? Could you perhaps manage with maybe a little less? Are all of the rooms really necessary? Do you really use all of the basement space now? And why do three of you need four toilets? Or one of you need three toilets? Smaller homes have granite counter tops too you know. And wood floors, so how about it?

O.K., so the area where you live is beautiful, and impressive, too.

"And really central, for just about everything," I hear you say.

Do you know something? I wish I had a dollar for every time I heard someone say that where they live is "really central."

Try it sometime. Ask your friend if where they live is really central. Everyone will give you the same answer. But don't laugh. They might get offended.

And so now, if you move, you can rest assured, knowing that your new location will be really central. Got the picture?

But, back to the point at hand. Is it really necessary for you to live where you do or could you downsize, just a bit? There may be two very good arguments to be made in favour and against so why don't we examine them closely.

To downsize. The advantages.

In this corner are:

More cost efficient use of space. In other words, getting full value from every square foot for your invested dollars.

A significant reduction in the operating costs. You will find less money being spent on heating, electricity, water and air-conditioning. (This will create savings that will go into your retirement plan).

Further savings will be made in reduced taxes - more money for your retirement plan.

Due to the reduction in the value of the property, your mortgage will likely be much less resulting in additional savings - more money for your retirement plan.

Due to the reduced size, you will likely experience a reduction in the painting and decoration of the property - more money for your retirement plan.

I don't think that we have mentioned the strong possibility that you may wind up having a smaller mortgage to manage – yes, more money for your retirement plan.

The insurance premium on a smaller property will likely generate savings - yet more money for your retirement plan.

But there must be some disadvantages. Let's take a look.

To Downsize. The disadvantages.

In this corner are:

Reduction of prestige for the family. (It needn't be that way. There are lots of beautiful smaller homes in lovely areas. And really central too).

The inconvenience of moving. (This can be a pain for sure. But think of the long-term gain. Think of all the extra money for your retirement plan).

The kids being moved from an area where they have their friends and their local school. (Maybe find a smaller home near your present location).

There may be a few other disadvantages too, like a one-car garage, less closet space and a smaller back yard, but you have to admit that there's a pretty good argument to be made for you to give serious thought to at least discussing a move with other family members. If you live alone, then your decision is nearer than you perhaps think.

Do you remember what I said at the outset of this book, in the first few chapters? Didn't I caution you that there would be hard decisions to make to secure a comfortable retirement? Well this is just one of those occasions. You can take the pain now or hold out until the later years to take the punishment and have all those regrets. The choice is yours. And remember, it's not so much the things that we *do* do that we regret in later years, it is the things that we *don't* do.

I repeat. The choice is yours.

WHAT IS THE PLEASURE?

For those of you who have children, you will already know of the enormous pleasure derived from seeing them grow from little helpless infants into energetic young people with minds of their own. Similarly, for those of you who are self employed with a successful business, you too have experienced the enormous thrill that comes from dreaming about growing your very own business into actually doing it and seeing the fruits of your labour come to being. Hence the expression, *"It is the hope of reward that sweetens labour"* – how true that is.

Many dreams come true every day for people with hope and imagination but you need first to create the dream by using your mind to conjure up something that you would like to see happen. Something such as a Retirement Plan.

The plan needs to be realistic, achievable and time specific, in other words, there needs to be a date established by which time the dream should be achieved. And certainly it needs to be achievable else you will be merely trying to grasp something that isn't there.

But it isn't just the fruition of the dream that will create a mental buzz for you. It will be the daily growth before your eyes that will stimulate the excitement within.

My good friend Angelo and his wife Maria have a winery in British Columbia but it wasn't always there. They married young and perhaps in part, influenced by their Italian upbringing, almost immediately knew that they wanted to grow grapes and make wine together. And so, they had a dream, but it needed some work and research if the dream was to be achievable.

They studied different types of grape vines and the types of soil needed to be successful. Maria had an accountancy diploma and so was able to develop a business plan. This needed to have realistic financial projections that would hopefully convince a banker to put up the money for the venture.

They visited many wine producers and learnt much about the culture of grapes until they felt ready to start. They also needed to study the markets so that their wine would be saleable.

After many months of looking at farmland and wineries and talking with hoteliers and restaurateurs, their plan was ready. Their dream had become more detailed and advanced until one sunny day they found themselves sitting beside each other in fine leather chairs across from a bank official. He seemed stern and was studying their business plan.

"Where do you intend obtaining your start-up vines from?" asked the banker.

"We have made contact with vineyards in France who have supplied them previously to Californians." Angelo replied.

"But what about the import restrictions regarding flowers, vegetables and plants?"

"We have completed our inquiries with the Canadian Department responsible for that part of our plan" Maria replied. "It is covered under section three of our business plan on page seventeen. It demonstrates that the authorities will grant permission and fully support our particular type of enterprise."

"Excellent." came the comment from the bank official.

"Well, since receiving your business plan some weeks ago, I have had the opportunity to study it carefully and to also discuss it with my colleagues".

"The bank is pleased to approve the loan you need to get you started."

"Congratulations Angelo and Maria, we look forward to working with you as your bankers and we wish you every success in this exciting project."

Maria and Angelo hugged each other and gladly shook the official by the hand.

"Thank you! Thank you so much" they both blurted, as tears of happiness swelled in their eyes.

But that was just the beginning and there was surely much hard work ahead of them. But their dream was on its way and as the years passed by, so their pride grew along with their dream and their vines.

Sales exceeded expectations. Their wine won awards and hotels and restaurants everywhere beat a path to their door.

Similarly, with your retirement dream, you will feel the excitement and pride that comes, knowing that in the beginning, the idea was only that – just a dream. A dream for you that one day you would be debt free and able to spend your retirement time however you wish with those you love.

The expression "No Pain, No Gain" comes to mind and in this regard it somehow seems appropriate. Without a dream there is nothing to look forward to and so nothing to gain your attention as the years go by. Without hope or ambition, what is life for? What is the point of living?

And so, make the sensible choice, Plan your Retirement, build your dream and enjoy the pleasure and excitement of watching it ripen and grow into the nest egg that you want so much.

The pleasure will be yours for the taking and as with Maria and Angelo, the wine will be yours for the tasting.

Chapter ten
RETIREMENT AT LAST

I'M RETIRED – Do I still need to save?

This book assumes that you are still working full time or have not yet arrived at retirement age. When you do retire, there will be a number of issues you will want to know about, some of which will surface afterwards. It would be remiss of me not to supply you with some information for that exciting part of your life, but so I can do that sensibly I first need to walk you forward in time.

Here you are then, older and on the threshold of retirement, and moreover, with a Retirement Plan intact and investment accounts reflecting balances like those you predicted many years ago during your prime working years.

We've come a long way together since those early days of you sitting there at the table working on the financial charts and grids as you prepared your Retirement Plan. It seems a lifetime ago. But plaudits to you - you have weathered the storm and dealt stoically with the various problems and the frustrations that you went through denying yourself those good times for the sake of having a debt free retirement.

Now however, you have a feeling of apprehension. Well that is natural and to be expected. After all, you have never been here before and as with anything new or untried, you'll sense a curious feeling of nervousness as your mind is racing with the many questions that you've been asking yourself for years.

Unfortunately they will continue to remain unanswered for the moment and the purpose of this final chapter is to address those issues and to provide you with some practical solutions.

Here is an example of some of the concerns that you will likely have:

How much money will I now need to retain in my savings accounts?

How much money will I be able to withdraw from my investment accounts each month?

How long will my money last me?

Will I continue to need a fund manager?

Will I continue to need life insurance?

The answer to the third question will of course very much depend on the answer to the second question because if you withdraw too much from your accounts too soon your money won't last you very long. Without a portfolio of course, you will no longer have a use for a fund manager.

This may seem obvious to you but to their great surprise, many people have found themselves caught up in the euphoria of total freedom from work and consequently they overindulge with this newly found abundance of carefree days with nothing to do. This sad behaviour results in spending too much of their nest egg too soon and at all costs you need to avoid placing yourself in the same dilemma. But being the sensible person that I now know you to be, there is no likelihood of that I feel sure. And as the title of this book urges you *"Don't Outlive Your Money,"* it is part of my work to provide you with sensible guidance and answers so as to avoid that catastrophe.

To help you more easily find some of the answers that you now seek in your retirement years you could start by continuing to use the graphs and charts provided throughout the book and then of course work your way through from there.

IMPORTANT POINT

WARNING!

DO NOT OUTLIVE YOUR MONEY

By now, you should know that there is much speculation in the global village about the pension shortfall that many, if not most Canadians will have when they come to retirement. In fact, it is generally assumed that the entire experience of retirement will change radically in the near future.

It is predicted that retirees' federal pension levels alone will not provide them with sufficient incomes for them to live on and so many seniors will need to continue to work in some form or another for as long as they are able. As we have discussed, the age of sixty-five will no longer signify the common retirement age, as governments will find it necessary to withhold the distribution of pensions until a later age.

The phenomenon of an enormous group of aging people born between 1946 and 1964 will leave fewer people in full-time employment who will be able to make contributions to the Canadian federal pension plan. This major shift in demographics will reduce the annual growth of that fund and serious action will be imperative to reduce the amount of dollars going out of the plan by way of pension payments. In part, that is why the retirement age will need to be adjusted.

HOW DID YOU DO? – Was the pain worth it?

Let us retain the thought that you are perhaps in your late fifties or early sixties and have followed a great deal of the advice in this book. In fact, you are feeling quite good about your present situation.

Well, how exactly did you do? You may not have amassed a fortune, but what you have is real and it is yours. Like me, many years ago you prepared a retirement plan and by exercising self-discipline on many occasions you stayed within your agreed budget.

You hired a dedicated fund manager and regularly monitored your savings accounts with such skill that you find that you no longer need to wish for a legacy or a big windfall to guarantee a happy, comfortable retirement for you free from money worries. On any day, one glance at your various investment accounts immediately tell you everything you need to know and provide you with the enormous pleasure you seek. To be debt free in your early sixties is within your grasp!

During the several years leading up to that point you will revise your financial plan commensurate with the changing times and so create a number of simple but effective financial graphs and grids with timely realistic projections.

Along the years, you have learned to be prudent in your decision-making and in particular, one of your decisions resulted in saving many thousands of dollars on the type of mortgage you arranged on your home.

You paid off your mortgage sooner than you had hoped for, which created significantly more savings for you. You sensibly downsized your house and as soon as it was practical to do so, you also downsized your car and both of these actions saved you many thousands of dollars in operational costs as well as a major reduction in interest payments.

Further, you sensibly made each car last a few years longer and this decision also paid big dividends.

SHOULD I RETIRE EARLY? – if a package is offered should I take it?

So here you are in your late fifties, about to retire a few years early from full-time employment, but you still have an abundance of energy and mentally. You're still highly motivated. An early retirement package has been offered to you at your workplace but you're unsure what to do. You wonder if you're ready to say goodbye to this engine room, this hive of activity that has been your home for who knows how many years?

Are you really ready to take early retirement? It's important that you never miss an opportunity to earn good money that you could add to your nest egg but it is equally important that you make the right decision. After all, the wrong decision at this time in your life could spell disaster. There would be no turning back. At this age, you only get one chance. At some point in your life the chance or ability to earn money will no longer be there for a variety of reasons. It could be a decline in physical health or it could be a major accident. And who knows? It might happen sooner than you think.

Hopefully though, neither will be the case, but while you are healthy and are able to earn money there is nothing wrong with continuing to do so. Resist the temptation to throw any opportunity away. Did you ever hear anybody complain of having too much money?

But back to what *you* should do. Your employer has offered you a package that includes you taking an early retirement. Let's review some of your options:

a)   Advise your employer that you have decided to decline the offer. Hopefully, you will be able to remain in your present capacity until you reach the official retirement age.

b)   Apply to stay on in a reduced capacity with fewer responsibilities and perhaps a lesser salary. Part time even.

c)   Take the early retirement package on offer and search for a job elsewhere.

The advantages of taking options (a) or (b) include your familiarity with the surroundings in your present job; there is a tendency to feel comfortable if you stay. The downside is that everyone knows who you are and what you have been doing for several years. If you elect to apply for a more junior post with fewer responsibilities you could feel embarrassed at times and humiliated too if you have a junior telling you what to do.

IMPORTANT POINT

REGARDLESS OF WHAT YOU ARE TOLD,

A COMPANY MONTHLY PENSION PAYMENT

USUALLY REMAINS A MYSTERY

UNTIL YOU ACTUALLY RETIRE!

Option (c) also has advantages. One is that you would know immediately how much your company pension plan would pay you every month. Another is that sometimes it is possible to stay in a job too long; therefore, before senior management can start to make your life difficult, you leave now before the atmosphere gets nasty, because it certainly can and it possibly will.

After reviewing your situation and all of the variables you may decide on Option (a), remain in your present job, and reconsider your options, a year at a time.

Alternatively, you may decide on Option (b), which in itself is not a bad option. Staying at your job in a reduced capacity has lots of advantages and that may be what you want at this time in your life. Just remember that any financial package on the table may be a one-time offer, never to be repeated. You might not be told this. Your supervisor might not even know, because company policies change. And next year things could be very different. Personally, I have known people who declined this option, only to regret it a few years later.

Or let us suppose that you decide on Option (c), that you leave, take the package and decide to search for some form of part-time occupation elsewhere. This can be daunting, particularly if you haven't conducted a job search for some years, so here are a few more things that you should think about.

PART-TIME JOB SEARCH –
   An opportunity to add to your nest egg
Looking for a part-time job at this stage in your life can really be a lot of fun. Think about it. Firstly, you're already receiving a company pension and maybe you received a lump sum as well, in some form of severance package, so you have a renewed feeling of financial independence and every day is suddenly available to you to conduct a job search. No more faking a sick day or time off for a dental appointment!

Also, for you, no more the daily grind of chasing other cars in long lines of traffic. You are beginning to sense a feeling of exuberance as you realize your stress level has diminished to an amazing new low.

You may decide to look for some voluntary work. This can be very rewarding, albeit unpaid, and while many men elect this option, the Statistics Canada records show that more women are likely to seek unpaid work, such as volunteering or care giving at this time in their lives.

I particularly recommend that you be careful how much of your savings or pension you spend during these early days, as you are receiving only a part of what eventually will become your final total income. With the extra time on your hands there will be a temptation to stop for coffees, linger over an unnecessarily costly lunch or to needlessly wander into stores and be tempted to spend part of your nest egg on unnecessary purchases. All of these activities will cost you money, so try to keep yourself otherwise occupied and, whatever you do, spend within your budget.

Regarding the job search. It might be useful, and certainly cheaper, if you could prepare your own résumé, perhaps in two or three different formats. You might be surprised just how multi-skilled you are when you put pen to paper and remember all of the various tasks you were assigned under the guise of a single job title. Try putting the emphasis on different skills in each of the résumés. Also, at this age, employment history is usually needed for only about thirty years. Be careful not to over-qualify yourself. You will likely have a tendency to do this due to the extensive experience that you have.

Your job search should start with the local papers, local magazines and local shops, because if you can find a job near where you live, you will avoid driving long distances to work. This reduction in travel will save you money on gas and wear and tear on your car, and you can leave later in the mornings and get home earlier in the afternoons. All of these suggestions are designed to maintain your new lower stress levels. It also reduces the risk of a traffic accident and your auto insurance company might consider a reduction in your premium.

You may choose to stay in your established line of work, with a different employer but you should not feel obliged to do so. Trying something quite different can be very refreshing and provide you with renewed vigour. If you are able to work different shifts, this too can be interesting. Are you already smiling at the new life you will have when you retire?

APPLYING FOR THE POSITION –
  Junior positions are less stressful
     When you see an ad for a job that you would like to apply for, carefully study the skills asked for in the ad. Make sure you include these same skills in your résumé. I am not suggesting that you write untruths but if your résumé doesn't provide the precise details called for, it is likely that your application will be discarded immediately – I've seen this happen. If the advertiser asks for a résumé to be faxed, then fax it. Do not deliver it personally or send it in the mail.

     Sometimes advertisers can judge your responsive behaviour as too independent and assume that if you are given the job, you will create your own procedures instead of following the company protocol. I have witnessed this reaction too, on many occasions.

     Remember, it is likely that you will be older than your new boss and they will want you to *follow* them, not lead them.

     When you go for an interview, remember to dress smartly – but not too smartly. You don't want to create the impression that you could buy the company (even if you could) and try not to be too nervous. It might have been years since you last went for a job interview and it's only natural to be nervous.

     Here's a small tip: telling your interviewer that you're nervous will help put you at ease. Usually, people are very understanding in these circumstances, so try to be relaxed, be honest, and don't feel disappointed if it takes four or five interviews before you land a job. Remember, as one door closes another one opens for you.

     A follow-up letter a few weeks after an interview can pay off too. Especially if the successful candidate has not worked out or has decided to leave for some reason.

MAJOR TRANSITION – Fearing the unknown?
     This early retirement period in your life is one of major transition. If you live alone then during your working life, the loneliness would have been less noticeable because you worked with people all day and developed relationships. But now, unless you interact with others socially, your day will consist of just you.

If you are a woman, you may already know that the number of women retiring from full-time work is increasing greatly every year. With their considerable pension benefits, women are now having a major impact on the decision-making process affecting Canadians. Manufacturers of goods and services are having to rethink and retool in response to this development, in part because retired women have become a major spending power.

If you have a spouse or a partner that you live with, that too may take some getting used to, especially if they also are at home every day. If you are both working you may have planned for one of you to retire first and the other a year or so later.

It may be that working on your Retirement Plan for several years has, to some extent, prepared you psychologically for this transition and everything will be just fine. But for many, major change is something they haven't experienced for decades and this particular phase could be a shock to them at a time in their lives when they are most vulnerable.

During this period, both minds and bodies are starting to decline and that is why a small amount physical exercise can benefit most people.

COMPANY TRAINING COURSES –
Help for retirement planning

Many large employers, government offices and large institutions now recognize the impact that major change can have on retirees and their families. Their Human Resources departments offer training classes to help employees prepare for retirement.

When I was due to retire, my brother-in-law who was already retired said to me one day,

"You know, Robert, I think the most important thing to remember when you are approaching retirement is not to fear it."

"Is that right, Henry?" I said.

"Yes. I meet a lot of retirees and quite a few tell me they were actually afraid of retirement, mainly because it was something unknown and they weren't sure what to expect. They certainly felt ill-prepared."

What he said seemed logical. Sometime later, when I thought about writing this book, I remembered that conversation and hoped that some guiding words would help those people who presently face their retirement with fear.

I now believe that if the Retirement Plan that I have written about is prepared and adhered to, it could have a direct benefit in preparing people psychologically for retirement. In doing so, it could definitely help them avoid what might otherwise be an unwelcome surprise. I hope it will.

SHOULD I CONTINUE TO SAVE? –For what?

When you actually arrive at this happy situation, retirement in your sixties, leaving behind your years of toil and now, starting to enjoy the lifestyle that you hoped for and prepared for, you wonder if you should continue to save. The answer is, "Yes, probably," but it will very much depend on how much you have saved, how much you intend to spend, and when you spend it.

IMPORTANT POINT

LIFE DOES NOT END AT 65

THERE COULD BE ANOTHER 30 YEARS

MAKE SURE YOU CAN AFFORD IT!

Let's take a look at come of the monthly costs that you might have shaken off during your latter working years.
  a. Mortgage
  b. Car payment # 1
  c. Car Payment # 2
  d. Children's costs

    e.   Redundancy insurance (possibly)

    f.   Life Insurance (possibly)

    g. Department Store card payments/debts

Remember, life doesn't come to a complete stop just because you retire. In fact, if you have followed the advice and established your Retirement Plan, your nest egg could have grown well. For you, a renewed life has only just begun and with so much to explore, there is much to consider about how to spend your time.

Just be aware that you have recently lost a big paycheque and your life could continue for another thirty years or so. *Do not outlive your money!*

This section includes a plan to help you budget throughout your retirement years, in some way, just as you should have done for the past several years. (if you followed the book guidelines).

Calculate the amount of your monthly income and create an expenditure budget that has a value less than your monthly income. If this is not possible, then talk to your fund manager and decide how to square the circle.

If you have taken early retirement, you may need to withdraw a small amount from your savings or investment funds as a temporary measure until all of your pensions take effect.

Regarding your various savings and investment funds. You should maintain a finger on the pulse. Stay focussed. Review them regularly so that you continue to know exactly how much you have and where it is. In particular, keep an eye on financial trends happening in the marketplace that might affect your nest egg. What I am suggesting is that you should follow the plan that you prepared and that so successfully brought you to your present retirement age. Now, extend it into your seventies and even into your eighties.

Remember the old expression. If you don't know where you are going, any road will take you there. You need to remember where you are going and how much the journey will cost you.

It is important that you remain on the path that you know and that you personally planned and that you know where you are going in the future. This will be easy if you continue to track your yearly income and expenditure.

RISK LEVELS – In retirement, should I reduce my financial risk?

You may wish to discuss with your fund manager the levels of risk that you are now carrying within your portfolio. While you were working, you had time on your side to recover from any collapse in the marketplace. You also were earning that big monthly income as a full time employee and so you were able to take more risk with your savings.

You also *needed* to take more risk so that your funds would grow more quickly and provide you with the amount you needed to meet your projected target. But now you have a reduced income and fewer years to make up any major losses that might occur in your investments that may result from a higher risk. It might be sensible to discuss with your fund manager the possibility of reducing the risk levels within your portfolio while continuing to remain diversified.

Medium or high risk levels are fine for investments when the markets are spiralling, but you can easily get caught up in the hype and imagine that the markets will always have one direction to go. Don't be fooled or misled. Don't be seduced into a false sense of security. Your current investment levels have not come about by making reckless, impulsive decisions. Follow your instinct and know that all good things will come to an end at some point – including bullish markets that create fast-growing investment funds.

Review your risk levels and at this time in your life, be content with lower growth. You can do without the worry and you might even sleep better at night. Keep in mind that "two percent of something is better than ten percent of nothing!"

Polly was out shopping with her friend Laura. During lunch Laura revealed to Polly that as she was now retired and receiving a regular pension she could see no reason for saving anything.

"After all," she said, "With my regular pension, the same money is going into my bank account every month, so why would I need to save anything?"

The problem here is that if she fails to save anything from her pensions and as well, has very little money saved elsewhere, then she could easily find herself with a problem if she was confronted with an emergency.

Hopefully she was making the point that, as she already has substantial savings, she could see no reason to save any of her monthly pension income.

A CARE HOME –
   A major cost for the future years
   In your retirement years, you will need to face up to realities and, as sensitive as it might be, you should give thought to what for some is almost unthinkable – to make some provision for the time when you are alone and incapable. It might come any time, not necessarily when you are old, and when it does, do you really want to be a burden on others if you can avoid it?

There are some wonderful modern facilities designed especially for seniors who can no longer care for themselves. They are fully staffed with qualified personnel and some are almost like hotels. But they can be expensive.

While you are still healthy and agile you may think it sensible to visit one or two to get an idea of the costs and the types of services offered. You can then build the cost into your future financial budget within your Plan. You may not like the idea *now* of moving into one of these facilities as, to you, the occupants may look terribly frail and old.

Overall, you may find the idea of moving into one of these facilities depressing, but if you have to in twenty or thirty years time, your senses may not be as sharp as they are now and you might just appreciate having someone nearby to look after you.

You will also be glad that you did review what was available, because some of the homes have a waiting list of several years. Your situation in the future might see you paying rent for where you live and your investment fund could provide the answer to facilitate your move.

During this time in our lives it is entirely natural to dwell on the past. This is mainly due to the fact that we have so much of it and few plans for the future.

Perhaps with the help of your Twenty-Year Retirement Plan that you revised when you retired, you will now see your future as more interesting, deciding to include important milestones in the appropriate years and able to cost and budget for them. Suddenly you can see more details of your life ahead of you than was possible before.

And so it is important to maintain and revise your Long Term Plan and segment it into five-year parcels. This will also allow you to continue to know how much money you have in your savings and where it is.

You will be able to continue to project and track the value and now of course, you will have the time to master the technique. You can include a projected cost for any possible nursing care services during the next thirty years or so.

What I am trying to point out here is that if you totally ignore all of the discipline and routines that you have learned from this book, you could do a lot of damage to your portfolio of funds – funds that have taken many years and much study to create. Yes, retirement is to be enjoyed but you should continue to exercise prudence, spend cautiously, and stay with the Retirement Plan that brought you to this point so successfully.

You can consider the Plan as a kind of safety net, always there for you to refer to and give you the answers you may be looking for.

MONTHLY EXPENDITURE BUDGET –
    Discretionary Expenditures

If you followed the guidance of this book during your working years, you prepared for yourself a Monthly Budget so you were able to monitor and control your expenditure. Hopefully, you found this method an effective tool and were able to contain your living expenditures well within your income. For ease of reference I have included a Monthly Budget appropriately adapted for retirement purposes.

Now that you are retired, examine your monthly budget and recalculate how much you need to cover all of your outgoing monthly costs.

There is a very good chance that each month you will not spend nearly as much as you did during your working life. As the years roll by you will probably find that you need less and less money for your personal living expenses.

The money that you spend on toys or a treat for the grandchildren is thought of as discretionary spending. Usually, the amount of that cost will equal what was left in the pot from the month before.

INVESTMENT FUNDS AND SAVINGS

The value of your investments and savings during your retirement years will depend very much on the age you choose to retire from full-time employment. If you choose to retire *later* rather than earlier, your savings will have had more years to grow and more time to increase in value. That's the temptation that lies in wait – work until sixty-five, get a part-time job, then sit back and watch the investments grow big.

But as the idea of saving for your retirement is to enjoy your savings, you may choose to retire earlier. That's fine too, providing your retirement plan indicates that it is safe to do so.

You should know that there are laws that govern what we can do with some of our pensions. If you are like most Canadians then you probably will be holding some of your retirement savings in a Registered Retirement Savings Plan (RRSP). Some RRSPs have a limited shelf life and at some point they must be cashed in or converted into an annuity. Another other option is to convert them into a Registered Retirement Income Fund (RRIF). Many people elect to transfer their RRSP into a RRIF and if you do this, in fact, you may not even see the money. In most cases it is merely a formal transaction carried out by signing some documents in the office of your fund manager. This is a very important point as the transfer must be enacted at a particular age in your life. Depending on our politicians in Ottawa or Quebec, the required age may change from time to time. See your investment fund manager for advice and they will be able to tell you the best option for your particular situation.

PROJECT THE GROWTH –
    How big will your investment tree grow?
    When I prepared my original Retirement Plan, interest base rates were around fourteen percent. I projected that my savings funds would grow by eight percent each year. I thought that I was being conservative in my projection and that my prediction would be about right. Of course, I found it necessary to revise the plan once or twice over the course of the next twenty-years due to the major drop in interest rates, also due to the world markets going into the doldrums.

IMPORTANT POINT

YOUR R.R.S.P. FUND WILL EXPIRE
(Currently - when you are 71)

YOU HAVE OPTIONS

SEE YOUR FUND MANAGER

PENALTIES ARE CHARGED IF YOU MISS THE DATE

    During this period, negative growth became the order of the day. Negative growth is a fancy way of saying that the values go down! When that happens you really appreciate being diversified, knowing that while some investments are falling in value, others will be rising, even if only a little. At these times you will be lucky if you can just maintain the status quo.
    When the base rate was around fourteen percent we were told that we would never see three or four percent interest rates again. This would have been bad news for a borrower of money, but I had planned to be a *lender* of money in my retirement, so I was looking forward to the higher interest rates that I hoped would prevail in my retirement years.

Alas, when things changed, interest rates dropped like a rock and so some major review of my plan became necessary if it was to remain a realistic retirement prediction.

The procedure that you need to carry out here is to project an interest percentage rate that seems appropriate, given all of the information that is current at the time. As you will be reviewing both your plan and the business news regularly, you will likely hear of any change in the base rate almost as soon as it happens and you will then be able to make any necessary adjustment in your plan.

It was about ten years before I retired that I needed to make my last adjustment to the interest rate on my Retirement Plan, although I suspect that it may have taken me ten years to learn the expertise.

Hopefully, with your experience, knowledge and instinct, as well as the help provided in this book, your choice of an interest rate projection will be more accurate than mine.

Next, you need to establish a percentage figure for the annual growth of your *savings*, and remember this is an *average* rate. Some funds will yield more than others of course and this is why it's important to diversify. That way, when some funds go down, others will go up. Overall, if you monitor the situation and, in consultation with your fund manager, make any changes necessary, the total average yield that you predicted as a percentage should materialise.

MONTHLY WITHDRAWAL AMOUNT

The purpose of this Long Term Financial Plan that you prepared when you were perhaps in your forties is now about to blossom. This is what you have been planning for. This is what will supplement your federal pension and any company or private pensions that you may have, and this is where you can allow yourself to get excited.

You are about to select a number that may provide you with an additional income every month. I say *may*, because if you can afford to, it would be prudent to leave your investments untouched during these early years of your retirement.

To estimate this number, you need to first look at the original number that you used to calculate the fund growth. If, for example, you have already projected that the fund growth will be five percent, you can't take out six percent or before long your account will be depleted. That option may be fine later when you are older, but it would be foolhardy to spend more than your income every month during these early years. If you need the money, better to get a part time job.

In my particular case, Polly and I agreed to choose five percent as the amount of money that we would withdraw each month. As it happened, the plan worked out to our advantage. When I retired we had no mortgage, we had no car payments, and we had no credit card payments. In fact, we were debt free. Hopefully, you will be in the same position.

Your main pensions will likely take effect when you become sixty-five. As you may secure some small part time jobs before then, there should be no need to withdraw very much from your savings except perhaps for vacations.

Remember, every little amount that you can leave in the fund in the early part of your retirement will continue to grow and compound, year after year, which means that you will be earning interest on the interest.

Furthermore, as we can now expect to live beyond eighty and possibly into our nineties, we definitely want to grow our investment tree as large as possible.

This small degree of constraint does not mean that you should regularly deny yourself things. It just seems sensible to remain prudent, continue to maintain an active Retirement Plan, and use the monthly budget as your measuring stick for your daily spending habits.

LIFE INSURANCE – Still a requirement?
In the days when you were working and you were in your forties or fifties and possibly had a family, no doubt the kids were still at home living with you.

Alex and Pat are neighbours and Alex said to me only last week that they must have provided their kids with a very good home because they didn't want to leave. Despite his protestations, I rather think that deep-down he and his wife still liked having them around the house.

Pat had always shared in their sports activities by providing the usual taxi service at all hours of the day and night and she and Alex both cheered the loudest at any event where their kids had taken part. They were always a close family and it showed in the way they loved their kids to bits and giving them the very best of everything. No wonder the kids never wanted to leave – and look at how much the kids saved by living at home. Now that would have been a golden opportunity for them to start a retirement fund, even at that young age.

Pat will be one of the first wave of baby boomers to retire and with her executive job, she will be bringing home a pension much larger than Alex's. This falls in line with a recent Statistics Canada report[1] that stated that *the first female baby boomers will start their transitions to retirement with far higher levels of pension coverage than earlier female workers, and the behaviour of baby-boomer women will greatly influence what Canadian retirement will look like in the future.*

You are probably wondering what all this has to do with insurance, but if you think of the family as a major responsibility then you will quickly realize why.

As a parent, you are responsible for ensuring that your children are provided with as much in life as you can afford. If you are a single parent, then the onus will be doubly burdensome.

Some of your kids' expectations are basic requirements such as a decent home, lots of love and cuddles, nutritious meals, sensible clothing and a good education. (Not necessarily in that order). While you are busy providing these necessities of life, you continue to go to work every day to pay for them, as well as to buy the things that you want for yourselves.

Children want other things, too, such as summer camp and sports equipment, bikes and skateboards, skis and ice skates . . . . The list goes on and on and if we can afford it and the kids enjoy the chance to achieve their potential it all seems worthwhile. Until you add up the cost! It is a huge amount of money to come up with, especially if there are several kids.

So what happens if tragedy strikes, as it can? Fortunately, most families escape unscathed and journey through life without

---

[1] New Frontiers of Research on Retirement, Statistics Canada

experiencing major house fires, motor accidents, a drowning or
tragic death through disease. But when a family is affected, then what?

They say that time is a great healer, and, it can be, but during
the interim the grieving process must be endured. It is at times like this
that a close, loving family is appreciated, together with caring friends.
But later, when the dust has cleared and the severest pain has subsided,
stark realization of the future sets in.

If a husband dies or becomes incapacitated, how will the wife
cope? How will the kids cope? How on earth will you manage on just
one salary coming in? Or if you are alone as a single parent and a child
is lost or disabled, how will you hold yourself together?

If there is an active insurance policy a substantial payout will
help. It cannot change the situation but it could provide the funding to
underwrite some of the preferred options for you.

So the question remains. As you are now retired and have a nest
egg to look after your needs, do you still need to buy life insurance
coverage and the protection it can provide? I know some people who
continue to pay a life insurance premium in their retirement and
wouldn't have it any other way. There are also many people who
consider it unnecessary. Depending on your particular circumstances,
there may be a need for insurance such as the house, car and other
important items, but life insurance?

Polly and I have discussed the issue of life insurance at length.
We feel that our savings and pensions are sufficient for one of us to live
on when something happens to the other of us, as it surely will at some
point.

Be sure to carefully examine your pension papers that you
received when your pension started. Read the small print. The value of
a monthly pension that you receive from a former employer may reduce
significantly when you die, to the point that the survivor might receive
only half or even less of the present amount. They may even be
required to receive a relatively small cash settlement.

The answer to whether or not you need Life Insurance when
you are retired is entirely up to you. You know your own circumstances
best. Study the amount of your monthly income, the source, your

investments, and the value and size of your home (after deducting any mortgage).

If the kids have moved out of the home and are self-supporting, you may no longer need to consider them in the equation. Also, study your particular level of personal risk. For example, do you spend as much time on the road driving and do you drive during peak hours? Do you or your spouse have a hobby that could be considered dangerous? Consider all of the options that you can think of and then speak to your investment adviser so that a sensible decision can be made for you.

If your informed decision is that you no longer need life insurance, then any financial savings resulting from not paying out the premium on a life insurance policy can be put to other good use.

LIFE EXPECTANCY – How long will I live?

Have you any idea how old you will live to be? We are told by experts that we are all living longer and that due to improved medications and medical science we should be able to overcome many of the ailments that in the past would have killed or crippled us.

We are also told that genes have a lot to do with it and so if you are a woman and your mother died when she was ninety-five years old, you might also expect to survive to that age and more.

We are told that the eighty-year olds should prepare themselves to live for another ten years at least and that the seventy-year olds can expect to live for fifteen years or so, while sixty-year old people can expect to live for another twenty-years plus. Of course, all of these predictions are based on many variable factors, but let's study what they are really saying.

If you assume that what you are being told is true, then that's fine, but what will the medical experts be predicting in ten or twenty years from now? If every ten years or so they extend your life expectancy by another three or four years, if you are sixty years old today you could reasonably expect to live for another forty years. Astonishing!

Certainly, you will hear that you are now eating more healthily, or at least, that more healthy foods are available for you to select, and you probably take a regular power walk around the block or the local shopping mall.

Perhaps your biggest problem is keeping your weight down. Maybe you only need to look at food and you gain five pounds. I know many people who do, but to generalise, if you can follow the advise that is published and broadcast and stay away from anything that causes stress, then whatever the length of your remaining life, it will probably be one of reasonable quality.

So for those of you who had planned to spend your last dollar as you inhaled your final breath, you are advised to keep on saving as you will likely have about thirty years of retirement in which you will need to provide the necessary finances to sustain yourself. If you deplete your savings accounts too soon, that could be a long time to wait in line at the Food Bank.

You should continue to maintain a long term, twenty-year plan with five-year segments. The Plan should reflect your living costs, commensurate with your income. To repeat what I said earlier, during the first several years of retirement it is imperative that your living costs be controlled so that, if possible, and except where it is required by law to do so, little or no income should be withdrawn from any of your savings accounts. Remember that life has not finished yet, it has just renewed. Hopefully, you will have many years in which your savings will have to keep you.

While you may want to provide a legacy to younger family members, your first responsibility is to yourself.

In any event, talk to your professional financial adviser. The patience, dedication and sacrifices that you have made over the years to get you to your present position were made with the objective of rewarding yourself with a long, worry-free retirement, not a short one.

You will have earned your retirement. I hope that this book will have helped you to get there. A retirement free from financial worries and with a decent sized nest egg that will pay for the things that you want out of life.

Remember the golden rule: spend your money as much as you want, but only spend as much as is necessary. As they say, "A fool and his money are soon parted." Do not outlive your money!

Publisher: Lulu.com